JOHN PEARSE MUSIC PUBLISHING, P.O. Box 265, Center Valley, PA 18034

Copy Editor	Felicia Knerr
Illustrations	Barbara Field
Photographs	Maureen Cirocco
Tablature Graphics	Kathie Linville
Typesetting	Mary Faith Rhoads
Layout	Barbara Field
	Felicia Knerr
	Mary Faith Rhoads

Editor	John Warde

ISBN 0-9617175-0-5
Printed in the United States of America

CONTENTS

INTRO

BUYING A GUITAR

Although it IS still possible to find fine guitars hanging on pawn shop walls, the best place to buy your first guitar is at a reputable music store. To a pawn broker, a guitar is just another item to be moved as quickly as possible, like a used stereo, a chain saw or a fishing rod, so he's not likely to know too much about how a guitar should be set up or to care if it has some disastrous fault that could render it unplayable. There are, of course, pawn shops who do specialize in instruments and who take a real pride in both the quality of their instruments and their after-sales service. (There's a terrific one in Tulsa!) But until you know just what to be on the lookout for in a used instrument, stick with an established music store whose ONLY business is the sale of musical instruments and accessories.

Not every music store, however, knows how to set up an instrument properly, so how can you select the right store? The Yellow Pages are a good guide. If a store advertises a teaching program, that's a sign that they know what they're doing, so is a mention of them being an authorized repair shop for a well-known make of guitar--Martin and Gibson repair shops have consistently high standards. Be cautious of stores that have a heavy discount policy or permanent sale signs. If a store is so interested in moving a high volume of merchandise out of the door then it's unlikely that they check it very carefully or are interested in providing after-sales service. As a general rule it is much better to pay a slightly higher price for an instrument that has been checked over and properly adjusted by a store that will stand behind their work than to get an unadjusted and impossible-to-play super discount deal from a store that can't wait to get you out of the door so that they can hard-sell the next unwitting customer. There is a professional organization, the National Association of Music Merchants, that encourages very high standards among its members. The NAMM symbol in an advertisement, therefore, is a good indication that the store is responsible and reputable.

All the foregoing having been said, you just may see what looks like a great bargain in a used instrument store, pawn shop or garage sale, so here are a few pointers. The list is not complete, so always try to have someone with you who knows what to look out for.

The Headstock
The headstock of a guitar is one of its weakest points. Check to see that it's not cracked. If it is cracked--even just a hairline--don't buy it. If it has been cracked and repaired, unless I knew the repairman personally I still would not buy the guitar.

The Tuners
The tuners should be in good workable condition. If the gears are exposed, see that no teeth on the cog are broken or deformed. Beware of tuners that stick at one particular spot or tuners that are so sloppy that the tuning buttons can be turned more than a quarter revolution without the gears moving the string capstan. Tuners are not very expensive and can be replaced, but you want to learn to play the guitar--not repair it.

1

The Neck

The neck should be straight. Actually there should be a very slight dip about two-thirds of the way along to accommodate the "envelope" of the string (the amount of space that a string requires when it is vibrating). Hold the guitar as you would a rifle, and sight along the neck, looking down toward the body. If the neck has any more than a very slight dip, beware! If the neck has a twist--even a very minor one--don't buy the guitar. Some guitars have a truss rod in the neck that is adjustable either at the headstock or, in the case of some acoustic guitars, through the sound hole. A competent repair-person can use the adjustment to correct a SLIGHT neck warp but never a serious bend or a twist. The truss rod system was never designed to correct neck warps, no matter what a store clerk may tell you. It was designed to put a loading on a neck to compensate for the pull of the strings and allow the neck profile to be slimmed down for faster and more comfortable playing. If the warp has been caused by an imbalance in this loading, it is possible to correct it, using the rod adjustment very carefully. Many times, however, the problem is made worse because the rod has been adjusted at some earlier time by someone who did not know what they were doing.

Fingerboard

The metal bars inlaid into the fingerboard are called frets. If they are severely worn you will need to have them replaced. This would not deter me from buying a guitar that was perfect in every other respect. Sometimes a fret will pop up slightly in the groove in which it has been set. If this happens it will affect the "envelope" of one or more strings and you will hear the buzz of the string hitting the fret as you play. To check for this, methodically pick the string at each fret down the entire fingerboard, a fret at a time. If a string buzzes or sounds strangely dead, there is probably a sprung fret. Not a serious fault--but one needing attention before you play the guitar.

Shoulder

Where the neck joins the body is called, naturally enough, the shoulder. This can be another weak spot. Gently try to move the neck forward and backward and look for movement at the joint. If there is any visible movement, I would not buy the guitar. Look, too, for any signs of repair. Remember what I said about headstock repairs!

Body

Beware of any obvious repairs. The odd crack in the soundboard, sides or back is not necessarily a reason for not buying a guitar--if it's been repaired well. It's a good idea to look inside an acoustic guitar with a small inspection mirror if repairs have been carried out. ANY crack should be reinforced by the glueing, along its length, of small wood "diamonds." The wood should be the same type as the damaged wood (for example, spruce on the underside of the soundboard, mahogany or rosewood for back or side repair). Steer away from any instrument that shows signs of a sloppy or careless repair.

Braces

The soundboard and back are supported by shaped strips of wood called braces. These can come loose and cause a variety of trouble from an annoying rattle or buzz when you're playing to the total collapse of the instrument! Hold the body by the neck, with your hand muffling the strings, and tap GENTLY along the line of each brace. Listen for a rattle. It's probably a loose brace. Another sign of brace failure can be distortion of the soundboard. Look at the guitar from a distance. Does the soundboard show undue signs of stress? Any acoustic will "belly up" behind the bridge to some extent but if this swelling is so pronounced that the bridge is visibly tilted forward or if the stress appears to be lopsided, the internal bridge plate and/or some braces might be letting go. Loose braces are not a reason to pass up an otherwise good guitar--but they will need expert repair and it's not a particularly cheap job.

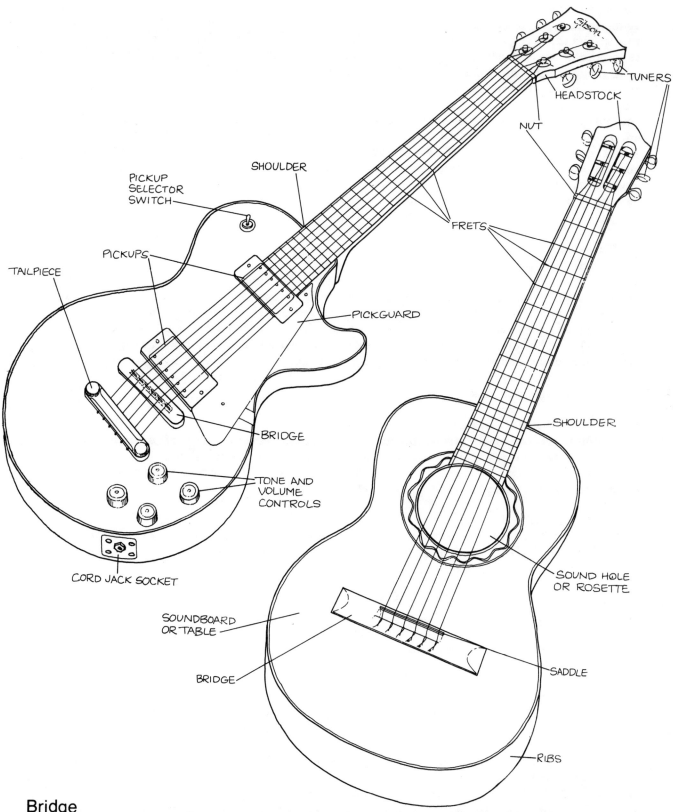

PICKUP
SELECTOR
SWITCH

SHOULDER

PICKUP

TAILPIECE

PICKGUARD

BRIDGE

TONE AND
VOLUME
CONTROLS

CORD JACK SOCKET

SOUNDBOARD
OR TABLE

BRIDGE

TUNERS

HEADSTOCK

NUT

FRETS

SHOULDER

SOUND HOLE
OR ROSETTE

SADDLE

RIBS

Bridge

The pull of the strings at the bridge can be around 150-160 pounds so it stands
to reason that difficulties can be expected in this area. Look at the juncture
of bridge and soundboard BEHIND the bridge. If there is a gap, the bridge will
have to be taken off, cleaned and reglued. Even if the salesclerk says that
it's been like that for years, remember what that string pull could do to you
if that bridge let loose without warning. Again, not a terrible fault, nor a
very costly repair--but one that would have to be carried out right away,
should you decide you want the guitar.

Electrics

If the guitar has a pickup system, make sure that you plug it into an amplifier and check it. Check that each pickup works. (If you're not sure which pickup you're hearing, tap it GENTLY with a flat pick.) Rotate both the volume and tone knobs to see that they function and look out for flat spots (controls that seem to affect the volume or tone only right at the end of their rotation). It could mean that you might have to invest in one or more replacement potentiometers (pots). If you hear a crackling or rustling noise as you rotate the controls it probably means that the pots are dirty. Energetically rotate the knobs back and forth a few times to see if that clears up the trouble. If they still crackle, it's a gamble. Applying a few drops of electrical switch cleaner to the pot spindle may eradicate the noise--or you may have to shell out for new pots. Unless the guitar is marvelous in every other respect, I would not advise taking a chance on a dodgy electrical fault.

STRINGS
Flat-Top Acoustic Guitar

In days long gone folks often strung their flat-tops with heavy gauge strings. Nowadays it's not necessary. String technology has advanced so far that medium or even light gauge strings can effectively drive the soundboard--and, thanks to great strides in microphone systems designs, even in an outdoor bluegrass festival, it's not necessary to torture the guitar with heavy strings in order to be heard on stage. The most popular strings are an 80/20 bronze wire or a phosphor bronze wire wound onto a steel core for the basses and plated steel for the treble strings.

Arch-Top Acoustic Guitar

The construction of an arch-top guitar necessitates the use of a much heavier string gauge than that used on a flat-top in order to move the arched soundboard efficiently. String composition is usually 80/20 bronze, phosphor bronze or nickel wound basses with plated steel trebles.

Electric Guitar

Electric guitars may be divided into two main types: guitars fitted with one or more magnetic pickups or guitars fitted with a piezoelectric pickup mounted beneath the bridge saddle.

For a guitar fitted with a magnetic pickup, the best string composition is nickel wound on steel core basses and plated steel trebles. The gauge of the strings is dependent upon the type of music to be played. Rock guitarists favor super light strings, often starting with .008 for the first string, while jazz guitarists invariably opt for much heavier strings (.013 is considered a light first string by many jazz players).

An instrument fitted with a piezo pickup is, in effect, an amplified acoustic guitar and would best be strung with 80/20 or phosphor bronze wound basses and plated trebles.

Classical Guitar

A CLASSICAL GUITAR MUST NEVER BE STRUNG WITH STEEL STRINGS!!!
A trifle emphatic, maybe, but at least I've gotten your undivided attention. Steel strings will ruin a lightly made classical guitar. It is just not made to withstand the pull of even extra light steel strings. Use a set specifically designed for the instrument, with silver plated wound bass strings and rectified nylon treble strings. Rectified just means that the string has been extruded (rather like squeezing toothpaste from the tube) at a slightly larger diameter than the gauge desired. It is then put through a series of grinding dies that mill it down to a perfectly exact gauge. Only in this way can you be sure of getting a classical treble string with a uniform diameter along its entire length, which is essential for accurate string intonation.

String Changing

You should never wait until your strings break from old age or become as dead as last night's spaghetti before you decide to change them. Guitar playing should be fun, and if you're cutting your fingers on rusty old strings or if your guitar "thunks" instead of "twangs," then you're just making learning that much more difficult. String changing isn't fun. I don't know anyone who LIKES to change strings, but it's not difficult and the difference in sound that a new set of strings will make on your guitar--and on your enthusiasm for playing --far outweighs the boredom of the actual restringing. Over the years I've whittled down my restringing time until I can change all six strings--and have the guitar back in tune--in under ten minutes! When I started out, however, it took me the best part of an hour.

Here are some tips.

First of all, buy good strings. Sure, you might be able to buy "El Cheapo" strings at 50 percent less than a good brand, but do you really want to have to change them in a few days when they break, go dead or play wildly out of tune? Get a GOOD set. They'll play truer, sound sweeter--and you won't have to change the darn things every other day. And get yourself a string winder!

This is a little gizmo with a handle and a cup that fits onto the button of the tuner. You just put the cup on the button and crank the handle to slacken off a string in order to remove it or to take up the slack when you're putting on a new string.

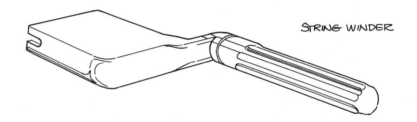

STRING WINDER

Try and get a winder with a pin puller slot in the cup. It'll save you much fingernail and fury.

Just flip your guitar on its back and lay it flat on your lap. Hold it firmly with your right hand, put the cup of the winder over the button of the string you're going to change first (I always start with the sixth) and crank the winder to loosen the string.

It's not a good idea to take all the strings off at once before you start to restring. It can weaken the neck. But about once a year I'll do it so I can scrape away the accumulated dirt from the fingerboard. I use a single-edged razor blade and then buff along the board and over the frets with fine steel wool to restore the board's smoothness and polish up the frets. Otherwise I ALWAYS change strings one string at a time.

Once you've freed the string from the tuner capstan, if your guitar has a pinned bridge, try to push the string down into the hole in the bridge. This will loosen the bridge pin and enable you to pull it out easily.

If it proves to be stubborn, take your string winder and slide the string puller slot around the neck of the pin and lever it out.

PIN BRIDGE

Try to push the string first. Your pins will last much longer if you don't have to lever them out each time.

Now, take your string out of the packet and unroll it CAREFULLY so that it doesn't kink--or take your eye out!

Feed the ball--the end with the brass bobbin--about an inch into the bridge pin hole and replace the pin behind it.

Seat the pin firmly, then carefully pull the slack out of the pin hole while holding the pin firmly in place.

Lead the other end along the guitar to the tuning peg and thread it through the hole in the capstan. Leave some slack to allow you to get a few wraps around, then lead it under itself to allow the coils to lock firmly when you tune the string up.

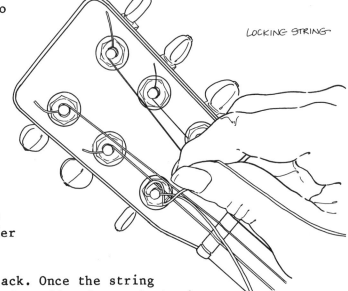

LOCKING STRING

Put your winder on the button and GENTLY wind the string while you take up the slack with your right hand. Try to get the coils to stack tidily on the capstan by guiding the string with your right hand. Also try to get them as low as possible in order to place less strain on the gears.

Only use the winder to take up the slack. Once the string starts to produce a note, take the winder off and tune by hand. It's much kinder to a new string.

Just before I tune up I usually grasp hold of the string just where it passes over the soundhole and--gently--pull it a few times just in case any windings have gotten hung up in the bridge pin hole.

Only when the string is up to playing pitch should you cut off the extra string hanging from the capstan. If you do it before, you could loosen the winding on the core and deaden the string.

If you have a classical guitar, begin to remove the strings in the same way, using the winder on the tuning peg. When the string has been freed, take hold of it about an inch from the bridge and push it through the hole to loosen it. It can then be removed. Next, take the new string from the packet and unwind it carefully. One end of a wound classical string will probably have a 1-1/2-inch section that is extremely floppy. Take the other end and push it through the bridge hole from back to front and--gently--pull the string through until only the floppy section remains behind the bridge.

Lead that floppy end up and over the bridge and lead it under the string where it exits from the front hole--

--then lead it back and down behind the bridge and under itself.

CLASSICAL BRIDGE

Finally pull the string in front of the bridge to take up the slack and lock it tight.

A nylon treble string doesn't have a floppy end, so you can use either end to thread through the bridge. I always tie a simple knot at the end, just in case it does decide to try to slip loose.

A nylon string is going to stretch out of tune when you first put it on. To minimize this stretching period I gently pull on the string rather as I would on a steel string that I wanted to free up in a bridge pin hole. Then I tune the string a half-tone higher than its proper pitch and leave it to stretch out for a couple of hours before I finally tune it to its proper pitch.

NAILS

The nails on your left hand should be trimmed very short so that your finger-tips can stand vertically on the fingerboard when holding down (fretting) strings. If a nail is allowed to grow past the end of your fingertip, it will cause that finger to lean over, preventing a good fingertip/string contact and maybe even causing the fleshy pad to touch and muffle a neighboring string. You'll find that guitar playing actually stimulates left-hand nail growth! The repeated compression of the tip as you hold down strings causes an increased blood flow to the nail root and your nails respond by energetic growth. Always keep some nail snips or scissors in your guitar case and make sure that your nails are trimmed back before you begin each practice session. Your right-hand nails should be allowed to grow past the end of your fingertip as you will be using them to pick the strings of your guitar.

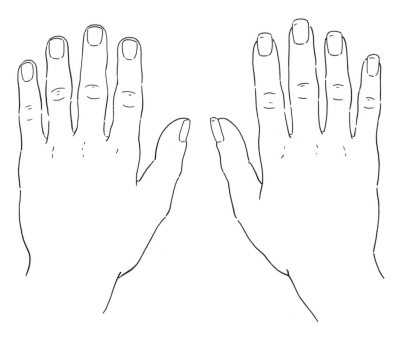

NAILS

Just how far past the end depends upon three things. The first is the shape of your fingertip. If, like me, you have stubby, square-ended fingers you'll need to allow slightly more nail length past the tip than you would if your finger-tip was gently rounded--otherwise you'll find that you are picking with the edge of your fingertip rather than the nail. The second deciding factor is the kind of music you want to play. A classical guitarist picks with a combination of fingertip AND nail, so his nails are only allowed to grow just past the tip--while a player of the "New Acoustic Music" or a ragtime player will very often play with just the nail so he--or she--will grow the nails up to 1/8 inch past the tip. The third factor is your nail strength. Some folks have very brittle or soft nails and so they have to keep them very short. If you suffer from either brittle or soft nails (I have dreadfully soft nails) you can either invest in some metal or plastic fingerpicks and a thumbpick--little gizmos that slip over your fingertips and thumb and enable you to pick the strings--or you can strengthen your nails by building up a number of layers of tissue paper

soaked in nail polish. For many years I used separated Kleenex layers and clear
nail polish, tearing the paper into 1/4-inch-square pieces, soaking them in
polish till they became translucent, and then layering them, one on the other,
on the nail until I had a lamination about five or six layers thick. Then I'd
seal it with a few coats of the polish. Now many nail polish companies are
making proprietary nail repair kits that work even better, as their tissue
paper seems to absorb the polish much faster. Every two weeks, when it begins
to discolor, I'll remove the laminate by rubbing it with cotton soaked in
polish remover--then slap on another protective laminate. I got this tip about
twenty years ago from the great flamenco guitarist, Paco Peña, and it's saved
me thousands of broken nails over the years. So pop around to your local drug-
store and see what nail repair kits they have. If you decide to go the Kleenex
route I would stick with colorless polish!

THE CAPO

The capo is a device that attaches to the neck of the guitar and clamps across
the fingerboard, holding down every string behind the same fret and thereby
raising each of their pitches by the same amount.

Each fret of the fingerboard raises the pitch of a string by half a tone, so,
for instance, a capo clamped behind the third fret raises the pitch of each
string by one and a half tones. The capo is a very useful accessory because it
can enable a guitarist to play in a number of keys simply by moving the capo to
different places on the neck. For instance, if you want to play in the key of
C, you could place the capo behind the third fret and play in the key of A, or
put the capo behind the seventh fret and play in G chords or, with the capo
behind the eighth fret, you could use the chords of the key of E. All will
produce the key of C.

Capos have been in existence for as long as stringed instruments. From carvings
and papyrus fragments we know that the Egyptians used capos apparently made
from animal sinew, which they bound tightly around the necks of their instruments, while the position marks on the fingerboard of a modern guitar are the
vestigial remains of the old European
tradition of boring holes right through
the fingerboard and neck of medieval
citterns to allow the fixing of a "bolt
and nut" style capo. This type of capo
was still in use in England in the
1700s on dittal harps and other
"romantic" parlor instruments played
by genteel ladies.

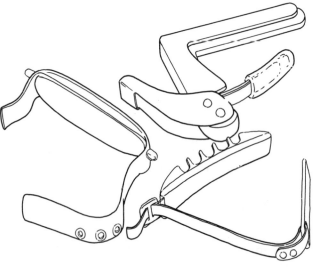

Nowadays there are dozens of different
kinds of capos to choose from. Some
screw on, others clip on. Just look
for one that isn't going to ding your
guitar when you use it. A good one is
the all-elastic Russell capo. Another
"kind-to-the-instrument" capo is the
one made by Jim Dunlop. Personally I
use either a Wilkerson or a Shubb because they are so quick to put on or
take off. Go to your local music store,
try out a few and see which you prefer.

CAPOS

CAPO POSITION TABLE

CHORDS IN THE KEY OF

	A	B	C	D	E	F	G
At the 1st fret	Bb	C	C#	Eb	F	F#	Ab
2nd	B	C#	D	E	F#	G	A
3rd	C	D	Eb	F	G	Ab	Bb
4th	C#	Eb	E	F#	Ab	A	B
5th	D	E	F	G	A	Bb	C
6th	Eb	F	F#	Ab	Bb	B	C#
7th	E	F#	G	A	B	C	D
8th	F	G	Ab	Bb	C	C#	Eb
9th	F#	Ab	A	B	C#	D	E
10th	G	A	Bb	C	D	Eb	F
11th	Ab	Bb	B	C#	Eb	E	F#
12th	A	B	C	D	E	F	G

FLAT PICKS

A great deal of guitar playing calls for the use of a plectrum--what pickers in the States call a flat pick or, sometimes, a straight pick.

'Way back in the old days flat picks were made either of tortoiseshell or nitrocellulose, both of which gave a really good sound. Nowadays, nitrocellulose has ceased to be used for picks because of its rather unpleasant habit of exploding violently into flame if exposed to heat (it's not used for movie film now either, for the same reason) and conservationists have, thankfully, got a ban on the use of tortoiseshell. Some tortoiseshell picks do get into the country illegally from Mexico or the Philippines and show up in music stores from time to time. If ever you're offered some, don't touch them. We have modern substitutes that sound as good, are much cheaper--and which don't encourage unscrupulous poachers who rip the shells off live sea turtles and leave them to die in agony.

Today, flat picks are made from plastic, nylon, viscoloid, stone or metal. (A few are made out of ivory--another protected material-- but these are O.K. They are made from recycled piano keys, or so we are told!)

TROUBADOUR MUSIC

PICK ASSORTMENT

PLASTIC   Personally I dislike plastic picks. They ARE inexpensive, but you get an annoying "click" everytime you pick a note. Also they often tend to have a slow "response" (the time it takes a pick to recover after being bent slightly while picking a string).

NYLON   Nylon picks are popular because they often have a slightly textured surface. Some manufacturers "shoot" the mixture with pumice, which makes the pick less likely to slip from your fingers, though the nature of the nylon itself does cause it to have an even slower response than a plastic pick. They tend not to click--unless they are very thin--but they DO have a picking sound --rather like a soft "tuck" that I find annoying at times. For electric playing, however, a nylon pick is very useful.

VISCOLOID   This is the same kind of stuff that picks used to be made from-- but it won't go BANG (another annoying sound!). Modern viscoloid has the fast- est response of any pick material and will give you the most efficient flat pick. I shoot my picks with a pumice and silica mixture, which speeds up the response still more, making them as fast, and as good, as tortoiseshell picks--and a lot easier to hang on to!

STONE   Over the past few years picks made out of agate have appeared on the market. They are too heavy for me, but a lot of jazz players swear by them. Jazz players tend to prefer a thick pick with no bend whatever--Django Reinhardt used to play with a horn trouser fly button!--and even today the gypsy jazz guitarists in Europe play with picks up to 1/8 inch thick!

METAL   Some companies now make picks out of copper. Again jazzers like the heavy gauges. I find, however, that the medium picks can crease and fold up, which can be embarrassing if it happens in the middle of a solo.

Picks come in every shape and color. I use either a small Jazz Pick or a slightly larger, asymetrical pick I designed some years back to give me three different playing contours--and thus three different playing sounds-- which I call the Studio Pick. Both of them are white viscoloid so I can see them easily should I drop one on stage.

JAZZ PICK

You should go to your friendly local music dealer and buy a selection of picks in different shapes, materials and thicknesses to see what feels good to you.

STUDIO PICK

1 TUNING UP

In every country where the guitar has established itself, you'll find "special" tunings. In West Africa, for instance, they will often tune the first three (treble) strings in standard tuning--but the remaining three strings will be tuned an octave (eight notes) higher than they would normally be. This they call "High Life" tuning. In Nashville many studio players tune almost the same way, except they raise the third string up a whole octave as well! They call this "High Strung" tuning. In Hawaii there are six or seven different tunings --one of which we'll be looking at later, while in England one of the most popular "modern" tunings for guitar is called DADGAD, after the notes to which the guitar is tuned.

The most widely used tuning, however, is called "Standard" tuning.

E A D G B E

Perhaps the easiest way to tune your guitar is to use pitch pipes.

Pitch Pipes

These look rather like a small harmonica and contain six reeds, each one tuned to a string of your guitar. While they are inexpensive they do have one slight fault. They can "blow out" of tune if you treat them roughly--so always blow them very gently.

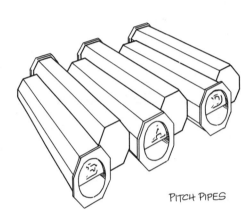

PITCH PIPES

You can see that the pitch pipe is not the perfect tuning method. It is, however, a good way to begin.

First of all, blow into the pipes to find the high E, then SLOWLY turn the first string tuning peg to bring the string in tune with the E pipe. Tune gently--don't force the tuning peg if it shows any reluctance to turn. If it doesn't want to move smoothly, put a drop of light machine oil on the gears, wait a few minutes, turn the gears back a quarter turn--and then continue tuning. As a general rule, it is easier to tune UP to a note rather than DOWN to it! The gears seem to bite better that way. When you're in tune, find the B pipe--that's the next lowest in pitch--and tune your second, the B string. Go from pipe to pipe tuning your strings until all six are in tune. Remember not to overblow the pipes or they will blow out of tune.

Noting

Pitch pipes are not always very accurate, as I told you, so what we need is a good way to check our tuning. It will also let us get in tune accurately if we can establish the tuning of just ONE string. If you want to play with some other pickers at a folk or bluegrass festival, for instance, and you can't stop them to ask if you can tune to them, if you can hear enough to let you go off and tune just one string to the pitch in which they're playing (they'll never be right at standard pitch--they'll always be a tad low or high) then, using noting you'll be able to tune all your other strings, using the one you've retuned as your guide.

Look at this. It's a diagram showing the first seven notes on each string of
your guitar.

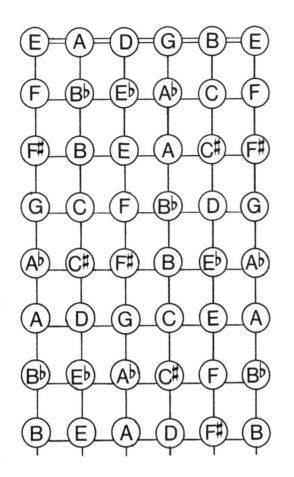
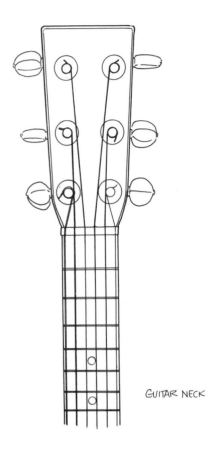

GUITAR NECK

Now look at your guitar. Along the fingerboard are metal bars called frets.

These frets are arranged so that they will raise the pitch of a string by ONE
HALF TONE each time you hold a string down behind a fret.

Now our first string is tuned to E.

Looking at the diagram, how many frets do we have to come up the second string
in order to raise its pitch from B to E?

Five. If we come up five frets on the second string, B, we change its pitch to
E--the same pitch as our first string played open.

Try it.

If the notes don't match, adjust the SECOND string.

When you're in tune, take a look at the diagram again and see how many frets
you have to travel on the third string until it produces the same note as the
open second string. Now the third string is G and the second is tuned to B--so
we must come up four frets on the third string to produce the note B.

Try it, and adjust the third string if necessary.

Now look and see how many frets you have to travel on the fourth string--D--in
order to produce the same note as the open third string--G.

12

Five. Adjust the tuning of your fourth string to bring it in tune with the open third string.

On to the fifth string. How many frets do we need to travel to bring it in tune with the open fourth string?

Five.

Finally, look at the diagram to see how far you must travel on the sixth string to produce the same note as the open fifth string.

Five. Match the notes and your guitar should be in tune.

HOLDING THE GUITAR

The Classical Position

Sit with your back straight and the body of the guitar resting on your left thigh.

The whole weight of the guitar is supported by the leg so that your left hand is left completely free to move about on the fingerboard.

You should raise your left foot up about five or six inches in order to bring the guitar's headstock to approximately level with your shoulder. For this you can rest your foot on your guitar case or on a brick, or you can do what I do whenever I forget to pack my footstool--which, of course, is another alter- native. I just lay my right foot over on its side and rest my left foot on it.

It works fine for short periods but can be aggravating for longer than four or five minutes.

CLASSICAL
POSITION

13

Jazz or "Folk" Position

In this position you sit, again with a straight back. The guitar rests on your right thigh, but even though the guitar neck angle is pretty well parallel to the floor you should take care that none of the weight of the guitar is carried by your left hand. To ensure that this doesn't happen raise your right foot--again, five or six inches--to lift the guitar up under your arm.

Classical players tend to dislike this position but many fine jazz and folk guitarists use it. I tend to switch between both positions so I'd advise you to do the same. For delicate, carefully articulated classical tunes I use the classical position-- but blues or ragtime just doesn't feel right if I don't have my guitar set firmly on my right knee!

One more thing. Don't use a guitar strap while you're learning. It really makes it difficult to develop good technique. Instead, invest the money in a new set of strings and wait until you've got through Lesson Thirteen. Then, if you find that you need a strap, get one that attaches at the end pin and the shoulder of the guitar rather than at the headstock. A strap attached at the headstock is always in the way and it puts a severe strain on the neck of the guitar. If your guitar doesn't have a strap pin at the shoulder, your friendly local music store will install one for you for a couple of dollars.

FOLK POSITION

CHORDS

There is no mystery to chords. A chord is just three or more notes that usually but not always sound harmonious when they're played together.

Building chords is as easy as ABC. In fact it's easier, because we don't use the whole alphabet--just the first seven letters, A to G.

Now don't get worried, I'm not going to make you read music. With my teaching method it's not necessary for you to read notation--but I'd like to show you how easy it is to build chords using the first seven letters of the alphabet.

When you were checking your tuning you probably noticed that there are only twelve notes, which repeat over and over into higher and higher or lower and lower octaves.

Here they are: A♭ A B♭ B C C♯ D E♭ E F F♯ G

When you get to G, you start at A♭ again--so we can, if you like, look at this cycle of notes as a wheel, with each step around it being one half tone.

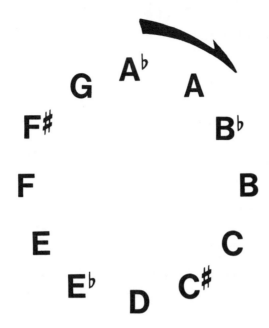

We build chords by choosing certain notes from that wheel, using very simple formulas.

First let's look at a scale.

A major scale, DO RE MI FA SO LA TI DO, is made from a fixed formula of half-tone and full-tone steps around that wheel.

Here it is.

TONE TONE ½ TONE TONE TONE ½

Suppose we want to make a scale in the key of G Major. We would start at G on our wheel and, going clockwise, using our formula, we would go one tone. Remember, each step is a half tone, so we would go from G to A.

Now we go another tone, which brings us to B.
Then we go a half tone, to C.
Then a tone, to D.
Then another tone to E.
Then still another tone to F♯.
Finally, a half tone, to G.

So the notes of the G Major scale are G A B C D E F♯ and G.

At the back of your book is a fingerboard chart. Turn to it and play a G Major scale on the first string, starting at the third fret.

How did you get on?

O.K. Using this simple formula you can work out how to play ANY major scale. Just choose your starting note and count 1 1 1/2 1 1 1 1/2.

15

So, now we have a scale, how do we get a chord?

Easy. We use another simple formula.   **1 3 5**

Look at the scale we just worked out.

If we take G as 1, what would 3 be?

B.

How about 5?

D.

So a G Major chord is made up from the notes of G, B and D. Now we know what the notes of a G chord are, here's how we play it.

A G chord is made up of G, B and D notes. So, using our left-hand fingers and the frets of the guitar, we have to change any string that isn't one of those notes into a G, a B or...you guessed it, a D.

Take hold of your guitar and we'll start with the first string, E. That's not a note that we need, so let's come up the neck until we get to a G, B or D.

F, F#, G.

At the third fret we have a G.
So we mark it on a diagram
called a chord window.

The easiest finger to hold
that note is your third finger.

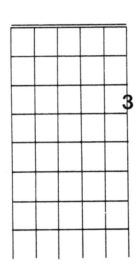

Now the second string is a B--
so we can leave it alone.

The third is a G--so that also
stays unaltered.

The fourth is a D--again
another note that we need in
our G chord.

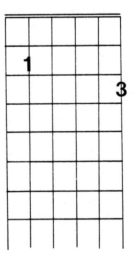

The fifth is an A. We'll have
to change it, so look for a G,
B or D.

The second fret gives us a B,
so let's mark it down on the
window. I'd use my first finger
to hold it down.

Which brings us to the sixth
string, low E. Come up three
frets and we get a G.

Mark it on your window, held
down by the second finger.

Last, we write the name of
the chord above it.

G MAJOR

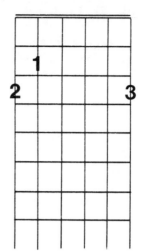

Now, let's check your fingering.
Make sure that just the tips of
the fingers are pressing the
string down behind the frets.
Play each string separately with
your right-hand thumb and listen
for buzzes or dampened strings.

If you do have a buzz, you're
probably not holding the string
down firmly enough--or you're too
far away from the fret. YOU MUST
ALWAYS HOLD DOWN A STRING
IMMEDIATELY BEHIND THE FRET.
If, on the other hand, you have
a string that sounds dampened,
look to see if another finger
is leaning over and touching it.

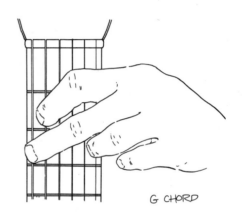

G CHORD

To get more pressure on the
strings, push your thumb against
the back of the guitar neck,
like this:

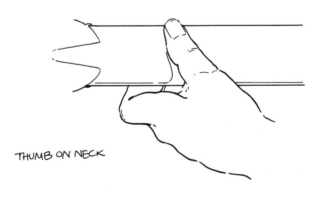

THUMB ON NECK

Practice _____

Draw out a tone wheel and then work out the G Major scale for yourself.

Practice holding down your G Major chord.

A NEW CHORD, D7

To find the notes we need for the chord of D7 we must first build the scale of D Major. To do this we use the TONE TONE HALF-TONE TONE TONE TONE HALF-TONE formula that you learned in Lesson One.

Here is the scale of D Major: D E F# G A B C# D

Check it on your tone wheel.

Now to find a dominant seventh chord we have another simple formula.
Here it is: **1   3   5   ♭7**

We just take the first, the third and the fifth notes like we did in order to make a major chord, plus we add the flatted seventh note.

So, the first is D.
The third is F#.
The fifth is A.
And the seventh is C#. However we want the FLATTED seventh. How would we flat a note? Well, all we do is play it one half tone--one fret--lower. So, instead of C# we play--you guessed it, C.

So the notes of a D7 chord are D, F#, A and C.

Let's build the chord.

Our first string is E, so we must change it to a D, F#, A or C.

At the second fret we have an F#, so let's hold that down with our third finger.

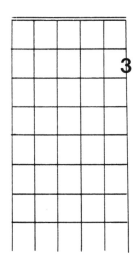

Moving on to the second string--B--we have another note that we must alter.

At the first fret we have a note--C--so we'll take it and hold it down with the first finger.

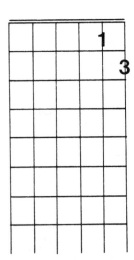

18

Third string is G, but
if we come up two frets
we find an A, which we
can hold down with the
second finger.

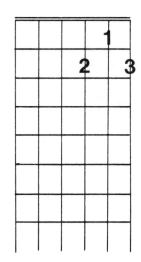

Fourth string is D, so
we don't have to change it.

Fifth string is A. Another
note that we need.

Sixth string is an E. We could change it, but, for now, we'll just not play the string. We show that on a chord window by marking an X above it--and we finish off the window by writing the chord name above it.

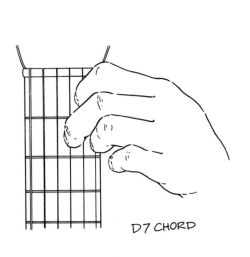

D7 CHORD

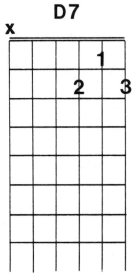

O.K., hold down the chord of D7 using the fingers I've recommended. As with the G chord, play each string in turn to make sure that each one rings out cleanly. Remember to "stand" each fingertip vertically on the fingerboard and get as close behind the fret as you possibly can.

Also, don't forget to push on the back of the neck with your thumb to help you push down firmly.

The next thing to do is to practice changing smoothly between the G chord and your new chord, D7.

Strum the strings with your right hand thumb. Like this:

    G chord   STRUM STRUM STRUM STRUM

    D7 chord   Don't forget to miss the sixth string.
                  STRUM STRUM STRUM STRUM

    G chord   STRUM STRUM STRUM STRUM

When you're changing chords try to move the fingers of your left hand all at once rather than moving one, then another, and so on. Lift all your fingers off the fingerboard and put them down in the new chord fingering. It'll take some practice, but if you work at it you'll soon get the hang of it.

Here's a song to help you work on those changes. The strokes under the words are strums by your right-hand thumb.

SKIP TO MY LOU

Chorus: G

HEY		HO,		SKIP	TO MY	LOU.	
1	1	1	1	1	1	1	1

D7

HEY		HO,		SKIP	TO MY	LOU.	
1	1	1	1	1	1	1	1

G

HEY		HO,		SKIP	TO MY	LOU.	
1	1	1	1	1	1	1	1

D7   G

SKIP	TO MY	LOU	MY	DAR	-	LING.	
1	1	1	1	1	1	1	1

1. I'll get another one prettier
      than you (X 3)
   Skip to my Lou my darling.
   Cho: Hey, ho etc.

2. Little red wagon, paint
      it blue (X 3)
   Skip to my Lou my darling.
   Cho: Hey, ho etc.

3. If you can't get a blackbird
      a bluebird'll do (X 3)
   Skip to my Lou my darling.
   Cho: Hey, ho etc.

4. If you get a good woman stick
      to her like glue (X 3)
   Skip to my Lou my darling.
   Cho: Hey, ho etc.

Practice the song through until the changes are occurring smoothly.

CARTER STYLE

'Way back in the twenties, folks across the country would rush to their local record stores to get each new 78 by a vocal group called the Carter Family. No other country group in history has had such an effect on the music of the United States, and their success was due in no small measure to the driving thumb and finger guitar style of Mother Maybelle Carter. Much of today's bluegrass guitar has developed from this technique. Here's how to play it.

You'll be using your thumb and your index finger.

Now, you can play with the bare fingers, pick with your nails or invest in the finger and thumb picks that I discussed in the section on "Nails," earlier in the book. I usually use a plastic thumb pick and my paper-strengthened fingernail.

Let's practice the right hand without worrying about holding a chord.

20

Here goes.

1. Thumb plucks the sixth string.
2. The BACK of the index fingernail grazes DOWN across the remaining strings.

The rhythm is 1 2 DUM-CHING.

Try it: DUM - CHING DUM - CHING DUM - CHING DUM - CHING

Here is your song again, with the Carter style marked underneath the words.

One is the thumb pluck, two is the finger graze.

SKIP TO MY LOU

```
G
HEY            HO,          SKIP   TO MY   LOU.
1     2     1     2     1      2      1     2

D7
HEY            HO,          SKIP   TO MY   LOU.
1     2     1     2     1      2      1     2

G
HEY            HO,          SKIP   TO MY   LOU.
1     2     1     2     1      2      1     2

D7                          G
SKIP   TO MY LOU   MY   DAR   -   LING.
1      2     1      2     1    2    1     2
```

You can practice your right-hand movements whenever you have a few spare minutes, even if you're away from your guitar. Just rest your hand on your thigh or the edge of a table and "pluck" with your thumb, then "graze" with your index finger. Concentrate on making the movements as fluid as possible.

The more relaxed your hand is, the longer you'll find that you'll be able to play--and the better your music will sound.

Practice _____

Draw out a blank chord window covering the first TWELVE frets of the guitar. Mark the name of each string along the top nut, then write in the note produced by each string at each fret.

Practice "Skip to My Lou," using the Carter style. Try to keep the rhythm steady and don't take it too fast.

3 CARTER STYLE VARIATION

One of the marks of a good guitar player is his or her ability to provide an interesting accompaniment to a song. To this end, here is a variation on the Carter style that can provide a nice rhythmic texture to your accompaniment.

Hold down a G chord.

1. Thumb plucks a bass string, say the sixth.
2. Index fingernail grazes DOWN across the remaining strings. Then it grazes back UP.

Both fingernail grazes take the same amount of time as the original single graze. So the style is still 2/4. If we call the sound of the basic Carter style DUM-CHING, then we could call this variation DUM-CHINGER.

It's not necessary to graze back up across more than two or three strings; in fact, when I'm playing a fast tune, I will often only catch the first string on the up graze. Even so, it's enough to add an interesting texture.

Play the Carter style variation using the following chord sequence.

G	1	2	1	2	1	2	1	2
D7	1	2	1	2	1	2	1	2
G	1	2	1	2	1	2	1	2
D7	1	2	1	2	1	2	1	2

Keep your rhythm nice and steady and don't tense your right hand.

As your thumb plucks, curl your index finger into your palm ready for it to begin its downward graze--so that the whole movement of thumb plucking, finger curling, finger grazing down and then up leads smoothly into that finger curling into the palm as your thumb plucks again. Never be too eager to speed up.

Throughout these lessons you'll notice I stress that the most important thing in guitar playing is not speed but smoothness. If your playing is relaxed and fluid, then speed will come naturally, without your having to force it. It is now, when you're just starting out, that you should be trying to develop an approach to your playing that is as relaxed as possible.

O.K. rest your fingers for a while and let's build a new chord.

The Chord of C Major

Together with the chords of G Major and D7, the chord of C Major makes up what we call a BASIC CHORD SEQUENCE in the key of G Major.

Turn back to your tone wheel and, using your TONE TONE HALF-TONE TONE TONE TONE HALF-TONE formula, work out what are the notes of a C Major scale.

In fact, when you have a few free minutes, it's really good practice to sit down with your tone wheel and a piece of paper and work out the scales of every major key. Start at Ab and go right 'round the wheel, writing out the notes that make up each scale. Once you have these scales written out, you'll be able to use them to build ANY chord that you'll ever need.

O.K. What notes did you get for a C Major scale?

Here's what you should have: C D E F G A B C.
If you got something different, go back and see where you went wrong.

Now, do you remember how we find the notes of a major chord, using the notes of the scale?

Right, we use our 1 3 5 formula.

So C is our one note...
E is our three note...
...and G is our five note.

Let's work it out on the guitar.

The first string is E, so we'll have to leave it alone.

The second string is a B, so we'll come up just one fret to make a C--and we'll hold it down behind the fret with the first finger of the left hand.

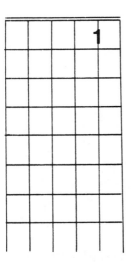

The third is a G--so we can leave it.

The fourth is a D, so we must change it to C, E or G.

If we hold it down behind the second fret we'll get an E, so let's do that--and we'll use the second finger.

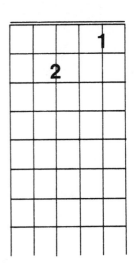

Which brings us to the fifth string, which is an A-- another note we'll have to change. How about coming up three frets to give us a C? Fine, use your third finger to hold it down.

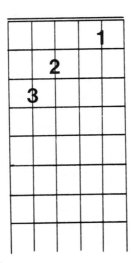

The sixth string is low E. As with our D7 chord, for now we're not going to play on that string--so we mark an X above it.

C MAJOR

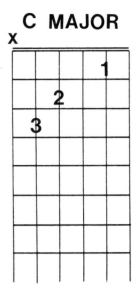

C CHORD

E is a note in the chord of C, but sometimes you find that you'll come across a note in a chord that your ear will reject--even though it is right. Low E in this C chord fingering is such a note.

Try playing each string of the chord in turn--including that low E and you'll see what I mean.

Now I said at the start of this section that G, C and D7 made up a chord sequence in the key of G.

Try it for yourself, using your Carter style variation.

```
G    1   2   1   2   1   2   1   2

C    1   2   1   2   1   2   1   2

D7   1   2   1   2   1   2   1   2

G    1   2   1   2   1   2   1   2
```

There's a basic chord sequence for every key and there is a simple-to-remember formula to show you just what chords make up that sequence.

1 4 5^7

So if we didn't already know what the basic chord sequence in the key of G Major was, we would simply write out the scale notes.

Do you remember them?   G A B C D E F# G

Then we would take the first note, the fourth note and the fifth note--as a seventh chord.

So, one is G...
...four is C...
...and five is D. However our formula is 1 4 5seventh so our five must be D7.

Carter Style $\frac{4}{4}$ Variation

Another Carter style variation is this one, in 4/4; four beats to the bar.

1   2   3   4   1   2   3   4 etc.

Hold down a G chord.

1. Thumb plucks a bass string, say the sixth.
2. This time the index finger grazes UP.
3. Now the index finger grazes DOWN.
4. Finally the index finger grazes UP.

There are four distinct beats...1 2 3 4 1 2 3 4 etc.

...make sure that you keep the rhythm steady; there can be a tendency to speed up on the upward grazes.

Notice, too, that for smoothness your index finger should be UNCURLING--ready to graze up--while the thumb is plucking the first beat.

As always, the best way to learn any new style is to put it into a song--so, here's "Skip to My Lou" again.

In addition to our new 4/4 variation, which I've marked beneath the words, I've also put in your new chord, C Major. You'll also see some numbers in circles ABOVE the words. They're to show you what string you should play with your thumb in order to play an "alternating bass line."

Instead of just plonking away on the same bass string all the time, you'll find that varying your bass line will add still more interest and variety to your accompaniment.

SKIP TO MY LOU

ⓖ   ⑤   ⑥   ⑤
G
HEY   HO,   SKIP TO MY LOU.

1 2 3 4   1 2 3 4   1 2   3   4   1 2 3 4

⑤   ④   ⑤   ④
D7
HEY   HO,   SKIP TO MY LOU.

1 2 3 4   1 2 3 4   1 2   3   4   1 2 3 4

⑥   ⑤   ⑥   ⑤
G
HEY   HO,   SKIP TO MY LOU.

1 2 3 4   1 2 3 4   1 2   3   4   1 2 3 4

⑤   ④   ⑤   ⑥
D7   C   G
SKIP TO MY LOU, MY   DAR   -   LING.

1 2   3   4   1 2   3 4   1 2 3 4   1 2 3 4

25

How did you get on?

Each Carter style variation stands on its own as a good accompanying "lick"--
but, for the best and most effective accompaniment you should experiment with
mixing them. You could do this, for instance.

Play the first line with the first Carter style.

Then the second using the 4/4 variation.

Play the third line using the first style again.

Then mix them on the last line.
Start with the 4/4 variation and end up with the 2/4.

SKIP TO MY LOU

⑥   ⑤   ⑥   ⑤
G
HEY   HO,   SKIP   TO MY   LOU.

1   2   1   2   1   2   1   2

⑤   ④   ⑤   ④
D7
HEY   HO,   SKIP   TO   MY   LOU.

1 2 3 4   1 2 3 4   1 2   3   4   1 2 3 4

⑥   ⑤   ⑥   ⑤
G
HEY   HO,   SKIP   TO MY   LOU.

1   2   1   2   1   2   1   2

⑤   ④   ⑤   ⑥
D7   C   G
SKIP   TO   MY   LOU, MY   DAR   -   LING.

1 2   3   4   1 2   3 4   1 2 3 4   1 2 3 4

Practice

Using the tone wheel, work out the major scale in the key of D. Then, using the
1 4 5seventh formula, work out the basic chord sequence.

Practice the 2/4 and 4/4 variations and switching between them and the basic
Carter style while you're playing the song.

Practice your new chord, C Major, and also practice changing between it and the
other chords of the basic chord sequence in G.

TUNING BY HARMONICS

Perhaps the most accurate way of getting in tune is to use harmonics--what the French call "Flageolet Tones."

For example, if you lightly rest the pad of a fingertip on a vibrating string at exactly halfway along its vibrating length--in other words exactly halfway between the nut and the bridge saddle--you will hear a clear, bell-like tone, a harmonic. Look at this.

When an open string is picked, the only two places that do not vibrate are those at either end of the string.

We call these places nodes.

Now, if you lightly place a finger on the string at the exact halfway point...

...you establish a third node, causing the string to vibrate in two equal sections. As these sections are each half the length of the original vibrating string, they each produce a note that is an OCTAVE ABOVE the original note.

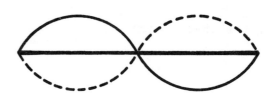

Theoretically, harmonics can be produced at ANY fractional division of a vibrating string--1/2, 1/4, 1/8, etc.--but many of them are inaudible to all but the keenest ear and, as such, are not really usable.

We can, however, use some of the audible harmonics to help us tune.

Tune your sixth string, low E, using a pitch pipe.

Now, touch your finger pad to the SIXTH string just over the FIFTH fret, pluck it--and then lift the finger away slightly.

Did you get a harmonic?

If you didn't, try it again. You don't have to pluck the string hard. Be gentle.

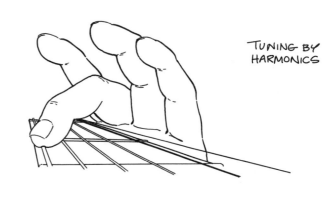

TUNING BY HARMONICS

O.K.?

Right, now touch the FIFTH string just over the SEVENTH fret and pluck it.

The two harmonics should sound exactly the same. If they don't, then adjust the FIFTH string tuning.

Next, ring a harmonic on the FIFTH string at the FIFTH fret and match it with the harmonic you get on the FOURTH string at the SEVENTH fret.

Again, adjust the FOURTH if they don't match.

Using the same fret harmonics, check the
FOURTH and THIRD strings.

Here's a diagram of what we've done so far.

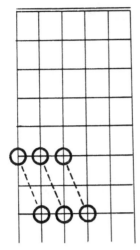

The next harmonic breaks
our pattern, because this
time we have to ring it
on the FOURTH string over
the FOURTH fret.

This is not an easy
harmonic to produce, but
you can do it. We match
that against the harmonic
on the SECOND string
over the SEVENTH fret.

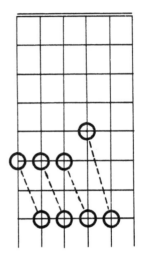

Right, back to our pattern again.
Match the SECOND string harmonic
over the FIFTH fret with the FIRST
string harmonic over the SEVENTH fret.

You should now be perfectly
in tune.

Here's a diagram of the full harmonic tuning.

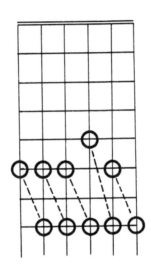

A New Key, D Major

If you worked out the scale of D Major as I asked you to at the end of Lesson
Three, you should have these notes written down:

D E F# G A B C# D

--and, if you went ahead and applied our 1 4 5seventh formula, then you already
know that the basic chord sequence is:

D G A7.

We already know how to play the chord of G--so we need only to build the chords
of D and A7.

We'll start with D Major.

How do we work out which notes make up the chord ?

We use our 1 3 5 formula.
One is D.

Three is F#
Five is A.

So we must change the pitch of any string on the guitar that is not a D, F# or
A to one of those notes.

Here's the chord window for the chord of D Major.

See if you can work out just what note each finger is holding down.

How about the first string?

F#

How about the second string?
Second string open is B, so
at the third fret it would be.....D.

The third string is....A.

The fourth string is open and is, of course, D.

The fifth string is also open and is A.

The sixth has an X marked above it.
That's because we're not going to play
it for the moment.

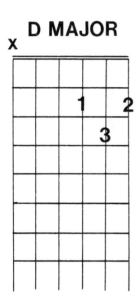

Take your guitar and put your fingers on the chord.

Remember to brace your thumb against the back of the neck of the guitar.

As with any new chord, pick each string to make sure that it is ringing
cleanly. To stop any string buzzes, your fingers as close behind the frets
as possible.

O.K., now the second chord we have to learn is A7.

If you refer to your tone wheel, you'll see that
the notes of an A Major scale are:

A   B   C#   D   E   F#   A♭   A.

By applying our 1 3 5 ♭7 formula we get A, C#,
E plus ...what would a flatted A♭ note be?

Well, flatting means that it should be a half
tone lower in pitch.

So, coming down the tones we have C B B♭ A A♭ ...G.

So the notes of an A7 chord are A, C#,E and G.

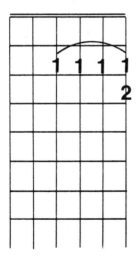

We use only the first two fingers to play this chord.

The first finger lays across the first four strings just behind the second
fret, rather like a stick. (To help you get good pressure on the strings,
really brace your thumb behind the neck.)

Now, the second finger frets the first string, just behind the third fret.

As always, play each string in turn to make sure that you have no buzzes or muffled strings.

Now play over the chord sequence to familiarize yourself with the changes.

Use your Carter style 4/4 variation, like this.

```
D    1   2   3   4   1   2   3   4

G    1   2   3   4   1   2   3   4

A7   1   2   3   4   1   2   3   4

D    1   2   3   4   1   2   3   4
```

O.K. Let's look at the right hand for a while.

A 2/4 Pick

Up till now we have been playing styles where a finger has been grazing across the strings. Guitarists call styles played like this "licks." Now I'd like to show you a couple of "picks"--styles in which the fingers pluck--or pick--the strings.

We'll start out with your fingers in the Spanish position.

Rest your index finger on the third string.
Rest your middle finger on the second string.
Rest your ring finger on the first string.

This position allows us to pick ALL THREE treble strings at one time.

Try it.

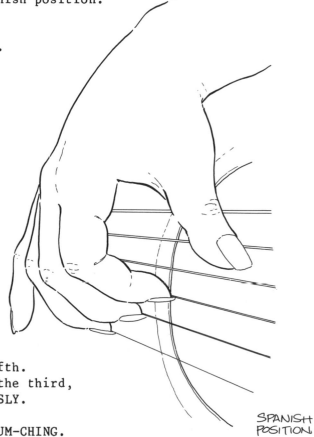

SPANISH
POSITION

If your fingers snag on the strings you're probably "grabbing" them. You shouldn't get under them and then pull them up toward your palm. The movement is more a pick ACROSS the strings.

Right, now...hold down a chord of D Major.

1. The thumb will pick a bass string.
   In the chord of D, we'll take the fifth.
2. Index, middle and ring fingers pick the third, second and first strings SIMULTANEOUSLY.

This is a 2/4 pick, so the sound should be DUM-CHING.

    1   2   1   2   1   2   1   2   etc.

A 3/4 (Waltztime) Pick

With the fingers still in the Spanish position, play this sequence.

Hold down a D chord.

30

1. Thumb picks a bass string, say, the fifth.
2. Index, middle and ring fingers pick the third, second and first strings.
3. Index, middle and ring fingers pick the third, second and first strings.

The pick is a waltztime--3/4--pick so the sound should be DUM-CHING-CHING.

    1 2 3 1 2 3 1 2 3 etc.

As always, it's easier to learn a new style or chord sequence if you put it in a song--so here's one in waltztime.

I've marked the rhythm under the words--1 is your thumb, 2 is a pick with the fingers, 3 is another pick with the fingers--and over the words I've marked suggested bass strings for your thumb.

Play it over slowly, paying particular attention to both the chord changes and the rhythm.

DOWN IN THE VALLEY

```
        ⑤                      ④         ⑤          ④
        D
        DOWN   IN    THE    VAL - LEY
Rhythm  1      2     3      1 2 3 1 2 3 1 2

               ⑤                         ④         ⑤          ④
                                         A7
        THE    VAL - LEY   SO     LOW
Rhythm  3      1     2     3      1 2 3   1 2 3   1 2 3

        ⑤                      ⑥         ⑤          ⑥
                               G          A7
        HANG   YOUR  HEAD   O  -  VER
Rhythm  1      2     3      1 2 3   1 2 3   1 2 3

        ⑤                      ⑥         ⑤          ④
                               G                     D
        HEAR   THE   WIND   BLOW
Rhythm  1      2     3      1 2 3   1 2 3   1 2 3

        ⑤                      ④         ⑤          ④
        D
        HEAR   THE   WIND   BLOW,  LOVE
Rhythm  1      2     3      1 2 3   1 2 3   1 2 3

        ⑤                      ④         ⑤          ④
                               A7
        HEAR   THE   WIND   BLOW
Rhythm  1      2     3      1 2 3   1 2 3   1 2 3

        ⑤                      ⑥         ⑤          ⑥
                               G          A7
        HANG   YOUR  HEAD   O  -  VER
Rhythm  1      2     3      1 2 3   1 2 3   1 2 3

        ⑤                      ⑥         ⑤          ④
                               G                     D
        HEAR   THE   WIND   BLOW
Rhythm  1      2     3      1 2 3   1 2 3   1 2 3
```

2. If you don't love me,
   Love whom you please.
   But throw your arms 'round me
   And give my heart ease.
       Cho: Give my heart ease, etc.

3. Roses love sunshine,
   Violets love dew,
   All the angels in heaven
   They know I love you.
       Cho: They know I love you, etc.

4. Gonna build me a castle
   Forty feet high
   Just so I can see you
   As you ride on by.
       Cho: As you ride on by etc.

5. Down in the valley,
   The valley so low,
   Hang your head over
   Hear the wind blow.
       Cho: Hear the wind blow etc.

A 6/8 Pick

Put your fingers in the Spanish position.

Hold down a D chord.

   1. Thumb picks a bass string, say, the fifth.
   2. Index finger picks the third string.
   3. Middle and ring fingers pick the second and first strings.
   4. Index finger picks the third string.
   5. Middle and ring fingers pick the second and first strings.
   6. Index finger picks the third string.

The style is in 6/8 so the sound should be DUM-ER-CHING-ER-CHING-ER.

   1 2 3 4 5 6 1 2 3 4 5 6 etc.

Here's the song again, written out for the 6/8 pick.

DOWN IN THE VALLEY

⑤   ④   ⑤   ④
D
DOWN IN   THE VAL   -   LEY
1 2   3 4 5 6 1 2 3 4 5 6 1 2 3 4 5 6 1 2 3 4

      ⑤   ④   ⑤   ④
                       A7
THE   VAL - LEY SO   LOW
5 6   1 2   3 4 5 6   1 2 3 4 5 6 1 2 3 4 5 6 1 2 3 4 5 6

⑤   ⑥   ⑤   ⑥
                 G   A7
HANG YOUR HEAD O   -   VER
1 2   3 4   5 6 1 2 3 4 5 6 1 2 3 4 5 6 1 2 3 4 5 6

⑤   ⑥   ⑤   ④
                 G   D
HEAR THE WIND BLOW
1 2   3 4 5 6   1 2 3 4 5 6 1 2 3 4 5 6 1 2 3 4 5 6

In the same way that we can mix together 2/4 and 4/4 styles to add interest to
a song accompaniment, we can do the same with our 3/4 and 6/8 picks!

DOWN IN THE VALLEY

⑤   ④   ⑤   ④
D
DOWN   IN   THE   VAL   -   LEY
1   2   3   1 2 3 4 5 6 1 2 3 4 5 6 1 2 3 4

      ⑤   ④   ⑤   ④
                        A7
THE   VAL - LEY   SO   LOW
5 6   1   2   3   1 2 3 4 5 6 1 2 3 4 5 6 1 2 3 4 5 6

⑤   ⑥   ⑤   ⑥
                   G   A7
HANG   YOUR HEAD O   -   VER
1   2   3   1 2 3 4 5 6 1 2 3 4 5 6 1 2 3 4 5 6

⑤   ⑥   ⑤   ④
                   G   D
HEAR   THE   WIND BLOW
1   2   3   1 2 3 4 5 6 1 2 3 4 5 6 1 2 3 4 5 6

⑤   ④   ⑤   ④
HEAR   THE   WIND BLOW,   LOVE
1   2   3   1 2 3 4 5 6 1 2 3 4 5 6 1 2 3 4 5 6

⑤   ④   ⑤   ④
                   A7
HEAR   THE   WIND BLOW
1   2   3   1 2 3 4 5 6 1 2 3 4 5 6 1 2 3 4 5 6

⑤   ⑥   ⑤   ⑥
                   G   A7
HANG   YOUR HEAD O   -   VER
1   2   3   1 2 3 4 5 6 1 2 3 4 5 6 1 2 3 4 5 6

⑤   ⑥   ⑤   ④
                   G   D
HEAR   THE   WIND BLOW
1   2   3   1 2 3 4 5 6 1 2 3 4 5 6 1 2 3 4 5 6

Practice _____

On a piece of paper, draw out a chord window for D7. Then, in a different
color, mark in the notes played by each fretting finger.

Practice your 2/4, 3/4 and 6/8 picks.

Review everything that we've dealt with so far.

5 TABLATURE

Tablature is the easiest way to write down just how both hands, working together, play music on the guitar. In fact, in this respect, it is a much better system than standard music notation. Standard notation is far superior for setting out the subtle nuances of a melody--but for "what finger do I use on what string at what fret and when?" you can't beat tablature--TAB for short.

Despite what some musicologists say, tab is a very old music system, maybe even older than standard notation. It's certainly at least four hundred years old, as it was used 'way back in the sixteenth century by Juan Carlos Y Amat in both his guitar and lute method books and it may, in fact, be much older.

Modern guitar tab is written on a stave consisting of six lines, one for each string of your guitar.

1st String————————————
2nd String————————————
3rd String————————————
4th String————————————
5th String————————————
6th String————————————

The top line is your first string, the next one down, the second string...and so on, down to the very bottom line, which is your sixth string.

So we have six lines, one for each string of your guitar--and on these lines, we mark behind which fret a string must be held down in order for us to play a melody note that we need.

Say, for instance, that we have a pluck on the sixth string, held down behind the third fret--we'd show that by marking 3, for third fret, on the sixth string line.

Now, say the next note is a pick on the third string played without any finger holding it down--in other words, played open--we'd show that by marking O, for open, on the third string line.

Are you with me so far?

Good. Now, how about if we wanted to play two strings at the same time. Say, the second string open--and the first string held down behind the third fret?

Easy. We just mark an O, for open, on the second string line--and then we mark 3, for third fret, on the first string line--directly above it so that both notes are on an imaginary vertical line. This shows that they must be played SIMULTANEOUSLY.

O.K.? So, what about your right-hand fingers? How do we show just what finger picks what string?

VERY SIMPLY! We mark them UNDER the tablature stave. For instance, we'd probably use the thumb to pluck a note on the sixth string--so we'd show that by writing a T, for thumb, under the sixth string note.

A third string pluck would likely be
played by your index finger, so let's
mark an I, for index, under the third
string note.

I'd probably use my middle and ring
fingers to pick the second and first
strings--so let's mark an M, for middle,
and an R, for ring, beneath the notes.

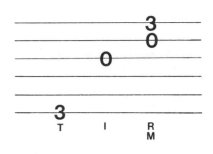

Now, to show that a chord is being held
down, we mark it ABOVE the stave...

For instance, a G chord.

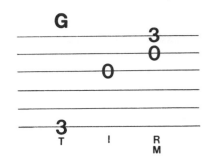

Get your guitar and play through to see
just what we've got written down.

Does it sound familiar?

It should. It's part of the 6/8 pick you
learned in the last lesson.

The whole pick would look like this.

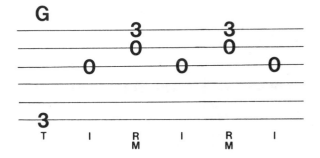

So, we know how to mark chords--and
fretting fingers--and picking fingers.
We now have to find a way to show rhythm.

To do this we first have to divide the
stave up into manageable pieces; as you
can imagine, it would be very easy to
get lost in a long rambling sequence of
notes. To divide up the stave we use
vertical lines called bar lines--and we
call the segments formed between two
lines, a bar.

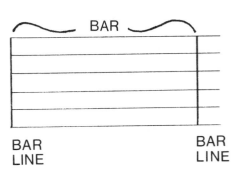

Here's our 6/8 pick again.

Because the pick is complete we have a
bar line at each end--and, to make the
picking easier to read, I've added some
links and brackets.

Sometimes you'll even see the rhythm
marked out below.

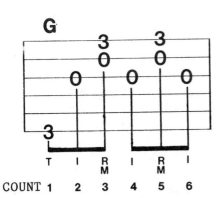

So much for our 6/8 style. What about Carter style; how would that look?

Well, it's a 2/4 style, so that means two beats--or counts--to the bar.

Let's use a G chord.

Again, we'll start off with a thumb pluck on the sixth string held down behind the third fret.

Then we have a graze down with the index finger that we show by means of a new sign--the brush.

If we wanted, we could play this 2/4 style through twice in each bar.

This would give us...

...a 4/4 bar.

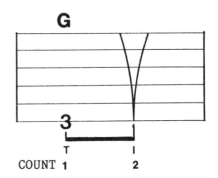

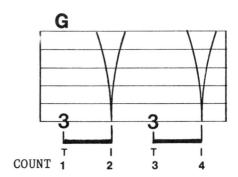

Here are all the other styles that you've learned so far, written out in tab.

2/4 CARTER STYLE VARIATION

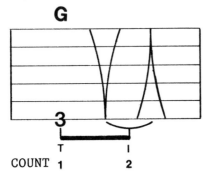

4/4 CARTER STYLE VARIATION

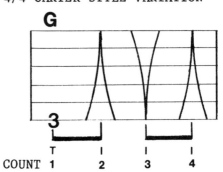

2/4 PICK

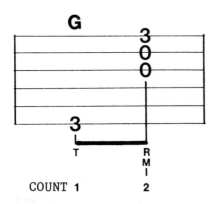

3/4 PICK

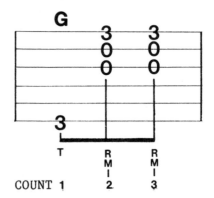

There are some other tablature signs but I'll show you those as we get to them.

An Alternative Fingering for G

You'll often be making the change from G to C, so, to make the transition easier, here is an alternative fingering.

In addition to making life a bit easier, this new fingering will build up the stamina of your fourth finger--your pinky. In guitar playing, we use that finger a great deal to play both chords and melody lines, so now is a good time to begin getting that wimpy digit in shape.

Hold down this new fingering.

Now change to a C chord.

Much easier, isn't it?

Practice changing between your new G fingering, C and D7.

G MAJOR

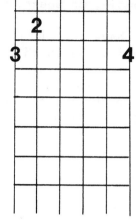

The Rocking Bass

A great deal of modern music is rooted on a bass rock that comes from the blues. Pete Seeger once said that you needed "an educated thumb" to play it.

Let's start that education.

Hold down a G chord. (Yep...your new one.)

There are four counts, or beats, to the bar, so we know that the rhythm is 4/4.

Pick your thumb on the sixth string. (It's marked to be held down behind the third fret, but your chord fingering is already doing that.) That's Count One!

Rock your thumb over onto the open fourth string and pick it. That's Count Two.

Now rock your thumb back onto the sixth string again. That's Count Three.

Finally, rock your thumb over onto the open fourth string once more. That's Count Four.

As you play it, count out the beats aloud. It'll help you to keep the rhythm steady. Tapping your foot also helps but it can become a habit that is very difficult to kick. If ever you work in a recording studio, NEVER tap your foot or the engineer will brain you. If he doesn't, the producer will! A foot tap will "leak" into any open microphone and can ruin a track--so it's best never to develop that habit.

O.K. Get the bass rock really steady because this is the foundation on which we are about to build our melodies.

Picking on the Beat

You can play a melody note on ANY or ALL counts of a bar.

For example, on Count One.

Here we have the first string held down behind the third fret and I'm using my middle finger to pick the note, simultaneously with the thumb--on the first count-- or beat--of the bar.

ONE 2 3 4
ONE 2 3 4
ONE 2 3 4 etc.

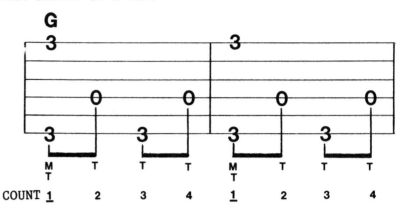

I can also play a melody note on Count Two. Like this.

1 TWO 3 4
1 TWO 3 4
1 TWO 3 4 etc.

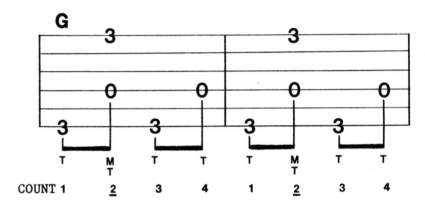

Here's a melody note on Count Three.

1 2 THREE 4
1 2 THREE 4
1 2 THREE 4 etc.

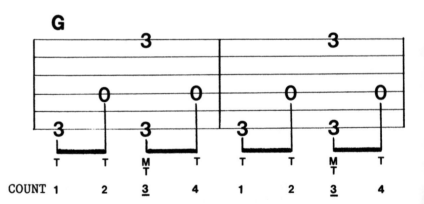

And, as you probably guessed, you can also play a melody note on Count Four.

1 2 3 FOUR
1 2 3 FOUR
1 2 3 FOUR etc.

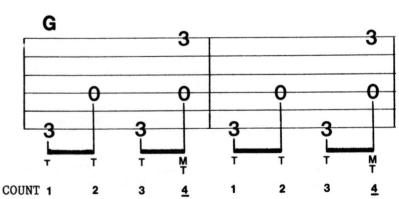

38

Sometimes you might even want to
play a melody note on EVERY count,
like this.

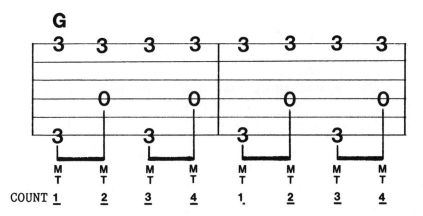

```
ONE  TWO  THREE  FOUR
ONE  TWO  THREE  FOUR
ONE  TWO  THREE  FOUR etc.
```

Before we go any further, go back over the tab explanation and make sure that
you really understand it--then practice the melody count bars until you can
pick, at will, a melody note on ANY count. An extra half hour or so spent on
really mastering this can save you HOURS of practice later on.

Starting a Tune

O.K. If you're ready, let's play a tune, "Bile 'em Cabbage Down."

B'ILE 'EM CABBAGE DOWN

Trad. arr. J. Pearse

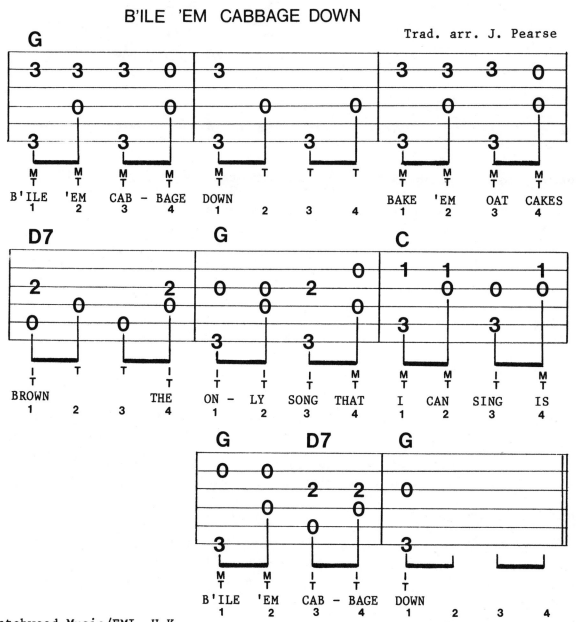

2. I used to live on a mountaintop,
   But now I live in town.
   I'm gonna buy me a beaver hat,
   And court Miss Sally Brown.
     Cho: Bile 'em cabbage etc.

3. I know she'll want to dance with me,
   When she hears my banjo ring.
   Oh, I could not be more happy,
   If I'd been born a king.
     Cho: Bile 'em cabbage etc.

4. I reckon she'll come back with me,
   To my little house of logs.
   She'll cook my food an' wash my
        clothes,
   An' whup my kids an' dogs.
     Cho: Bile 'em cabbage etc.

5. An' when my days are over
   She'll plant me on a hill.
   An' raise a marker over me,
   Shaped like a whiskey still.
     Cho: Bile 'em cabbage etc.

You should always look carefully
at a bar, before you plunge in to
play it, just in case there might
be an awkward fingering or some
other surprise lurking there--
so let's take the tune a bit
at a time.

Here are the first two bars.

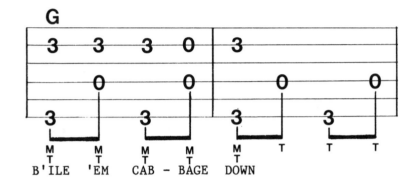

What would the rhythm be?

1 2 3 4 1 2 3 4. That's right, it's in 4/4--in other words, four beats,
or counts, to the bar.

Look for any chords you'll need to hold down--only one at present, G Major.

Now, will you need to move out of that chord fingering to play the bar?

Yes. There are melody notes on every count and to play the first three melody
notes you'll have to hold down the second string behind the third fret.

How would we best do that?

Easy! Just swing your pinky over from the first string, third fret, to the
second string, third fret. Remember to put it back afterwards.

Let's play Bar One.

Hold down your G.
Thumb plucks the sixth string held down behind the third fret. In the chord of
G that string is already fretted. You don't need to do anything except pick it.

At the same time, your middle finger picks the second string held down behind
the third fret. Swing that pinky over and play both notes simultaneously.

That's Count One.

Now, your thumb rocks onto the open fourth string and, again, your middle
finger picks the second string held down behind the third fret. (Where's your
pinky?)

That's Count Two.

Count Three is exactly the same as Count One, which brings us to...

...Count Four, which has the thumb completing its rock and ending up on the open fourth string. This time the middle finger picks the second string OPEN, so just lift your pinky off the string. Don't put it back on the first string just yet because you'll need it for the next note. Just lift it off--and play the open string along with the thumb rock on the open fourth string.

Try it.   1 2 3 4   "B'ILE 'EM CAB-BAGE"

Let's move on to the next bar.

It begins just like Bar One. Thumb and middle fingers picking on the sixth and second strings...don't forget to put your pinky back on the second string... then you just play the rest of the bar, using your thumb rock.

Try it.   1 2 3 4   "DOWN" 2 3 4

How did you get on?

O.K. Here are the next two bars.

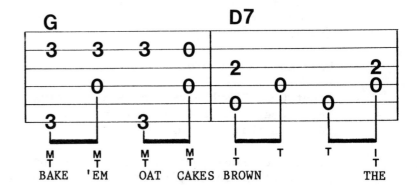

Bar Three is exactly the same as Bar One...try it...

        1 2 3 4   "BAKE 'EM OAT CAKES"

...so let's move on to Bar Four.

Here we are told to change to another chord, D7.

Count One. The thumb picks its first rock on the open fifth string, while the index finger picks on the third string held down behind the second fret. You'll notice that the D7 chord automatically frets that string.

Count Two. The thumb rocks onto the open fourth string.

Count Three. Thumb rocks onto the open fifth string.

Count Four. The thumb rocks onto the open fourth string again PLUS there's another index finger pick on that third string.

It goes: 1 2 3 4   "BROWN 2 3 THE"

Right, go back to Bar One and play through to the end of Bar Four. Don't be in a hurry. Remember what I said earlier about smoothness.

Practice _____

Throughly review the tablature instructions and practice the first four bars of the tune until you can play them through with no hesitation.

FINISHING THE TUNE

Here are the next two bars
of our tune.

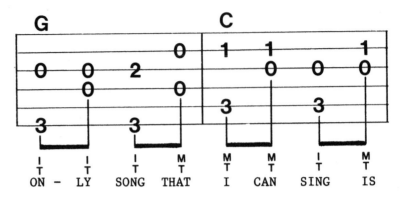

As always, check out the fingering. The first three melody notes in the first
bar are picked by the index finger. The last note is picked by the middle
finger.

Hold down a G chord.

Count One. Thumb picks the sixth string held down behind the third fret--your
chord does this automatically--while, at the same time, your index finger picks
the open third string.

Count Two. Rock your thumb onto the open fourth string and pick it together
with another index pick on that open third string.

Count Three. Rock your thumb back onto the sixth string once again. This time
the simultaneous index finger pick occurs on the third string held down behind
the second fret. The easiest way to do that is to swing your left hand second
finger across from the fifth--to the third.

Count Four. The thumb completes its rock by picking the open fourth string once
again. This time the middle finger picks the simultaneous note on the open
second string.

The whole bar sounds like this: 1 2 3 4 "ON - LY SONG THAT"

How are you getting on? Not so hard, is it?

Next bar. We have a chord change, to C Major.

Count One. The thumb begins its rock on the fifth string held down behind the
third fret--your C chord fingering will do that for you. It will also hold the
second string behind the first fret so that your right hand middle finger can
pick it.

Count Two. The thumb rocks over onto the open third string, while, at the same
time, your middle finger picks again on the second string, held down behind the
first fret by the chord.

Count Three. The thumb rocks back onto the fifth string once more, while, at
the same time, your index finger picks the open third string.

Count Four is the same as Count Two.

So, the whole bar is: 1 2 3 4 "I CAN SING IS"

O.K. Let's move on to the last two bars.

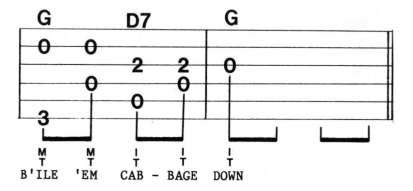

Hold down a G chord.

Count One. The thumb starts its rock on the sixth string held down by the G chord, while the middle finger picks the open second string.

Count Two. The thumb now rocks to the open fourth string while the middle finger again picks the open second string.

Change to a D7 chord.

Count Three. The thumb picks the open fifth string while the index finger picks the third string, held down behind the second fret by the D7 chord.

Count Four. The thumb completes its rock on the open fourth string while the index finger again picks the fretted third string.

Here's the bar: 1 2 3 4 "B'ILE 'EM CAB-BAGE"

Last bar of the tune.

Change to a G chord.

Count One. The thumb picks the fretted sixth string while the index finger picks the open third string.

If you were finishing the song there, that's all you would play. However, if you're continuing with other verses, rock your thumb through the bar on the sixth and fourth strings to bring you back to Bar One of the music again.

Go back to the start of the tune and play it through to get the picking--and the chord changes--SMOOTH!

A New Key, C Major
If you turn to the tone wheel, and use the TONE TONE HALF-TONE TONE TONE TONE HALF-TONE formula, you will find that the scale of C Major contains no sharped or flatted notes.

Here it is: C D E F G A B C

Now, using our 1 4 5seventh formula, we get the Basic Chord Sequence in the key of C Major.

1 is C, the key chord.

4 is F. You'll sometimes hear the 4 chord called the sub-dominant chord. If you hear someone talking about a sub-dominant chord, they just mean the 4 chord.

The 5 chord is G--but our formula calls for the 5seventh chord, so the 5seventh chord would be G7.

The Basic Chord Sequence in C Major, therefore, is C, F and G7.

How are you getting on with the formulas?

They're not so hard to remember, are they?

So, do you remember how to find the notes that make up each chord?

For a major chord, like C, we just take--which formula?

1 3 5. The first note of the scale, the third and the fifth.

So, the three notes of a C Major chord are C, E and G.

Now, you already know the chord of C Major, so let's move on to F Major.

Using the tone wheel and the TONE TONE HALF-TONE TONE TONE TONE HALF-TONE formula, we get the major scale:

   F G A B♭ C D E F.

Applying our 1 3 5 formula, we get the notes of the F chord.

   F A C

In order to play that chord on the guitar, we must change the pitch of any string that is not an F, A or C to one of those notes.

Here is a fingering for F Major.

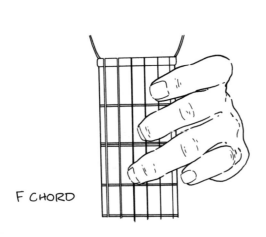

F CHORD

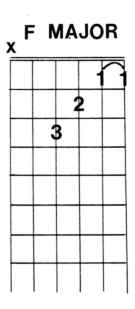

The first finger is holding down BOTH the first and second strings just behind the first fret.

The second finger is holding down the third string just behind the second fret.

The third finger is holding down the fourth string just behind the third fret.

The open fifth string is A, so we need not change it--and, at present, we will not be playing on the sixth string, E, so we need not alter its pitch either.

The third chord in our Basic Chord Sequence is G7.

Using our 1 3 5 ♭7 formula, you will see that the notes of G7 are:

     G, B, D AND F.

Here's the chord window.

The first finger is holding down the
first string just behind the first fret.

The second finger is holding down the
fifth string just behind the second fret.

The third finger is holding down the
sixth string just behind the third fret.

The second, third and fourth strings
(B, G and D) remain unchanged.

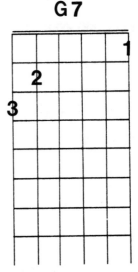

Practice

Spend as much time as you need in order to get 'B'ile 'em Cabbage Down" to a
stage where you can play it smoothly WITHOUT looking at the tab.

Practice the new chords in the key of C Major, especially the chord of F Major.

Draw out windows for both F Major and G7 and mark on them the notes played by
each finger.

7 "AND" COUNT SYNCOPATION

Not all melody notes fall tidily on one of the counts in a bar.

Some notes fall BETWEEN the basic counts, and these we call "and" counts.

We can pick a melody note, for instance, between Count One and Count Two, like this:

```
1& 2  3  4  1& 2  3  4
```

Or between Count Two and Count Three.

```
1  2& 3  4  1  2& 3  4
```

Or between Count Three and Count Four.

```
1  2  3& 4  1  2  3& 4
```

Or between Count Four--and Count One of the next bar.

```
1  2  3  4& 1  2  3  4& 1
```

To help you learn the rhythm, tap out the basic four counts on your knee with your hand.

```
1  2  3  4  1  2  3  4  etc.
```

Now tap your foot to the same rhythm. (Remember what I said earlier about not making a habit of this?)

```
1  2  3  4  1  2  3  4  etc.
```

Now count aloud the following exercise, tapping your hand along with your count, all the time keeping a steady 1 2 3 4 rhythm with your foot.

Here goes.

```
1& 2  3  4  1& 2  3  4  1& 2  3  4  1& 2  3  4
1  2& 3  4  1  2& 3  4  1  2& 3  4  1  2& 3  4
1  2  3& 4  1  2  3& 4  1  2  3& 4  1  2  3& 4
1  2  3  4& 1  2  3  4& 1  2  3  4& 1  2  3  4&
```

Count through five times.

Now try this.

```
1  2& 3  4  1  2  3& 4  1  2  3& 4  1  2& 3  4
1  2  3  4& 1  2& 3  4  1& 2& 3& 4& 1  2& 3  4
```

That's syncopation.

This is how we write "and" counts on a tablature stave.

We start off with our basic rock.

By the way, I'm varying the rock by swinging over onto the sixth string--it makes it more interesting. Just swing your third finger, left hand, over from the fifth string, third fret--to the sixth string, third fret. Don't forget to swing it back afterward.

By the way, do you know what note it plays when it's on the sixth string, third fret?

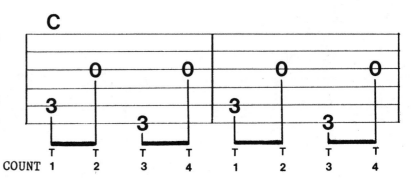

O.K. Here's an "and" count between Counts One and Two.

Try it.   1& 2   3   4   1& 2   3   4

A line is dropped from the "and" count to the bracket--then a link is put to one of the neighboring counts, usually the previous one.

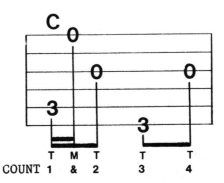

Here is an "and" count exercise to familiarize you with the syncopations.

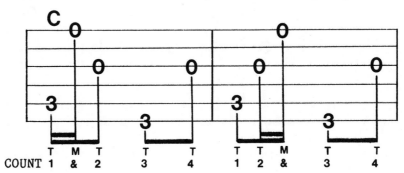

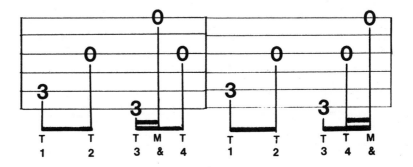

So, now you can play melody notes ON the beats, and melody notes BETWEEN the beats too.

You can also, in the same bar, pick some on and some between.

As ever, the best way to master a new guitar technique is to put it into a tune. Here's "My Home's Across the Blue Ridge Mountains."

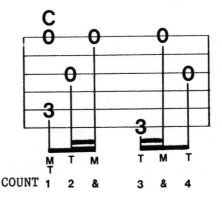

MY HOME'S ACROSS THE BLUE RIDGE MOUNTAINS

Trad. arr. J. Pearse

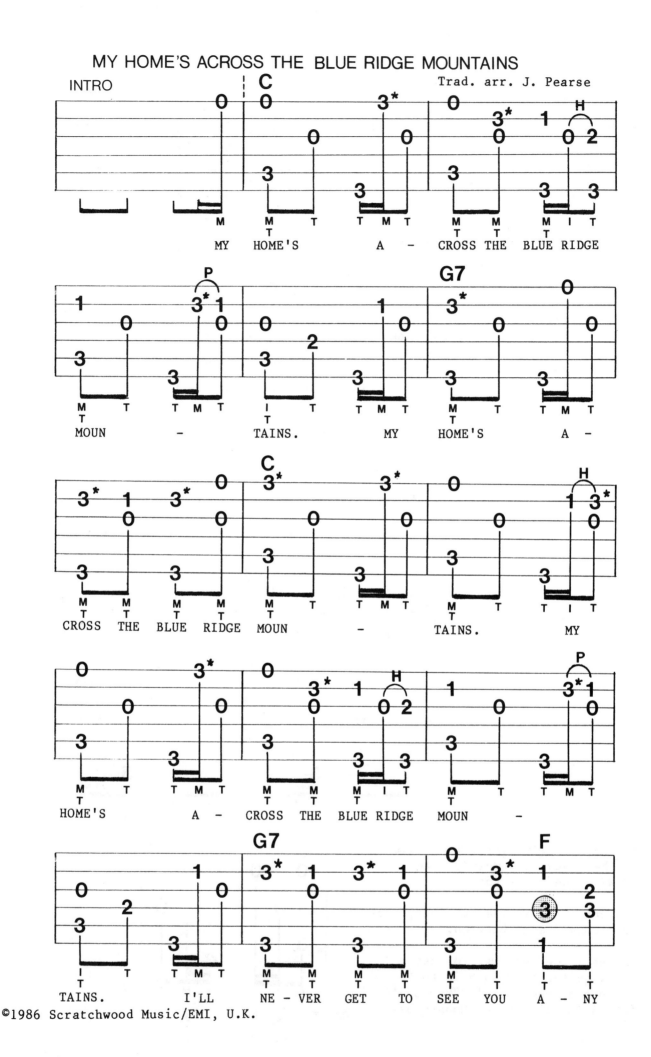

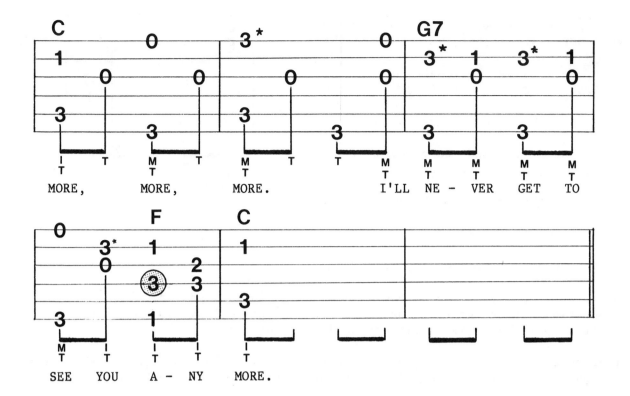

MORE,   MORE,   MORE.   I'LL NE - VER GET TO

SEE YOU A - NY MORE.

2. Where's the finger ring I gave you (x3)
   I'll never get etc.

3. Goodbye Darlin', Sugar Honey (x3)
   I'll never get etc.

4. My wagon's packed, I must be leavin' (x3)
   I'll never get etc.

5. My home's across the Blue Ridge Mountains (x3)
   I'll never get etc.

Don't panic--you can play it. However complex a tune might look at first, just remember that it's made up from a number of short bars. So...if we tackle them one at a time...we're sure to get through it.

Look at the first bar.

What would the rhythm be?

The giveaway is how the note is tied.

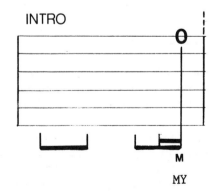

INTRO

MY

It's tied to the last of the four counts--so it's got to be an "and" count. As the other counts are silent, the rhythm is:

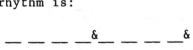

"And" Count. Middle finger picks the open first string.

That was an intro bar. The real melody begins when we're given our chord to hold down--so this is what I'll call the first bar, Bar One.

49

First, let's check out the rhythm. Look for the thumb rock, that will often give you your basic counts. How many are there?

Four. So we know that the tune is in 4/4. 1 2 3 4 1 2 3 4 etc.

Are there any other counts in there?

Yes, there's an "And" Count between Count Three and Count Four.

What does that make the rhythm of the bar?

     1 2 3& 4

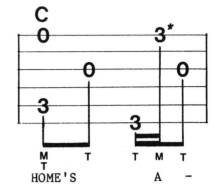

What else should we look for in the bar?

Well, any chord that we'll need to hold down, in this case a C....and what right-hand fingers we'll be using to pick out the melody. In the first bar we'll be using just the thumb and middle finger.

There's another new sign, too--an asterisk. That's the tab sign for your pinky. So any time you see an asterisk by a note, use your pinky to hold it down.

Hold down a C chord.

Count One. The thumb picks the fifth string held down by the chord behind the third fret at the same time as the middle finger picks the first string open.

Count Two. The thumb rocks onto the open third string.

Count Three. The thumb rocks onto the sixth string. (Don't forget to swing your third finger over to fret it.)

"And" Count. The middle finger picks the first string held down behind the third fret. Plonk your pinky down to fret it.

Count Four. The thumb rocks over onto the open third string once more.

Here's the rhythm.

     1 2 3& 4   "HOME'S A-"

Bar Two. First off, what's the rhythm?

1 2 3& 4, the same as Bar One. There's no chord change marked, so we keep holding down the C Major.

Count One is exactly the same as Count One in the previous bar. The thumb picks the fifth string held down by the chord behind the third fret, while the middle finger picks the open first string.

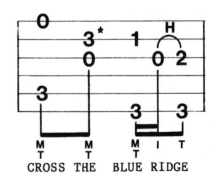

Count Two. The thumb rocks over onto the open third string at the same time that the middle finger picks the second string held down behind the third fret. Again, use your pinky.

50

Count Three. The thumb rocks back onto the sixth string again, but this time your middle finger picks the second string held down behind the first fret. Just lift your pinky up--and your C chord is already fretting the second string for you.

"And" Count. Here we come to a new sign, two notes linked by a bow with an H above. That is the sign for a "hammer on." It means that you play the first note and then, while it's still ringing, you hammer down on the string behind the second marked fret with a left hand fingertip. In this case, the index finger picks the third string open, then a fingertip hammers down on the string behind the second fret--I'd use the second finger to produce the second note.

Count Four. The finger should hammer on AT THE SAME TIME that the thumb is completing its rock over onto the fretted sixth string--so don't hurry the hammer on. Remember, the rhythm is "And Four", not "andfour." Two distinct notes MUST be heard.

Here's the whole bar: 1 2 3& 4   "CROSS THE BLUE RIDGE"

Right, next bar.

What's the rhythm?

Right, 1 2 3& 4.

Count One. The thumb picks the fifth string held down behind the third fret by the C chord. At the same time, the middle finger picks the second string held down behind the first fret, also by our C chord.

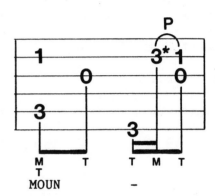

By the way, country pickers call this picking movement with thumb and finger a "pinch."

So, we pinch the fifth and second strings. Count One.

Count Two is a thumb rock onto the open third string.

Count Three is a thumb rock onto the sixth string again. (Don't forget to swing your third finger across in time to fret this string.)

"And" Count. Here's another new sign for you, two notes linked by a bow with a P above, signifying "pull off."

A pull off is the opposite of a hammer on. A finger frets a string which is then picked. While the note is still ringing, the fretting finger pulls slightly to one side in order to put more tension on the string, then it relaxes--allowing the string to slip loose--giving us the second note.

Pick--pull slightly to the side--let it go.

So, back to our tab. The middle finger picks the second string held down behind the third fret. As in the previous bar, I'd use the pinky.

Count Four. Now, while it's still ringing, pull it slightly to one side, then let the string pop free to ring the second note of the pull off at the first fret (held down by your chord, remember) AT THE SAME TIME as your thumb completes its rock onto the open third string.

Here's the bar: 1 2 3& 4   "MOUN---"

How about Bar Four?

Same rhythm as before, 1 2 3& 4, and there are no pitfalls to watch out for.

Still hold down your C chord.

Count One. The thumb picks the fifth string--held by your C chord--while the index finger picks the open third string.

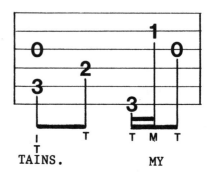

Count Two is a thumb rock onto the fourth string held down behind the second fret--again your C chord will do that. We're not rocking onto the third string this time, because we just played it and it would be an awkward movement if we played it again.

Count Three is a thumb rock onto the sixth string again. (Don't forget to swing your finger over.)

"And" Count. The middle finger picks the second string held down behind the first fret by your chord of C.

Count Four. The thumb completes its rock on the open third string.

The whole bar is: 1 2 3& 4   "..TAINS..MY"

Right. Go back to the intro bar and play through to the end of Bar Four.

Practice _____

Practice the "and" count exercise and then write out four bars containing random "and" counts (1& 2 3& 4 1 2 3 4& 1& 2 3 4& etc.) and play them over until you can play any sequence of "and" counts without faltering with your basic thumb counts.

Work on the first four bars of your tune.

8 FINISHING THE TUNE

How is the tune coming along?

It's surprising how easy it is if you just take it slowly, a bit at a time.

Here are the next four bars.

The rhythm of the first bar, Bar Five, is 1 2 3& 4.

Hold down a G7 chord.

Count One. The thumb picks the sixth string held down behind the third fret by your G chord. At the same time, the middle finger picks the second string held down behind the third fret. (I'd use the pinky.)

Count Two is a thumb rock onto the open third string.

Count Three is a thumb rock onto the sixth string again.

"And" Count. The middle finger picks the open first string. (In our G7 chord the string would be held down behind the first fret by your first finger--so just lift the finger up.)

Count Four. The thumb completes its rock on the open third string.

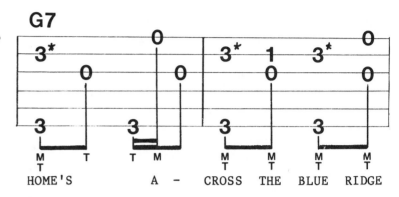

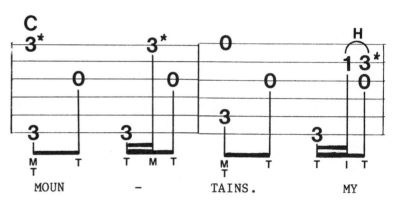

Here's the bar: 1 2 3& 4   "HOME'S A-"

So let's move on to the second bar, Bar Six.

We still keep our G7 chord but the rhythm in this bar is different.

It's 1 2 3 4--because there are no "and" counts marked.

It's a very straightforward bar. Try it for yourself.

     1 2 3 4   "CROSS THE BLUE RIDGE".

How are you getting on?

O.K. next, the third bar, Bar Seven of the tune.

Change to a C chord.

What is the rhythm of the bar?

Right! Back to 1 2 3& 4 again.

Try it for yourself: 1 2 3& 4   "MOUN---"

Next bar, the last one of this group, Bar Eight of the tune.
No chord change is marked, so we still hold the same chord, C.

How about the rhythm?

It's 1 2 3& 4--and we have a hammer on at the end of the bar.

On the second string held down behind the first fret--which it normally is when
you're holding a C chord--we have a hammer on from the first fret--to the third
fret. Use your pinky.

Here's the bar: 1 2 3& 4   "'TAINS..MY"

The next four bars should look
familiar.....

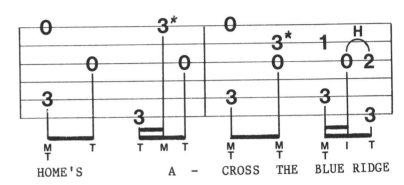

HOME'S   A - CROSS THE BLUE RIDGE

...because they're played exactly
the same as the first four bars of
the tune.

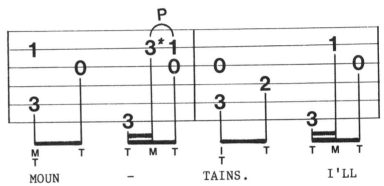

MOUN   -   TAINS.   I'LL

So, let's move on to the NEXT four.

Change to a G7 chord for the first
bar, Bar Thirteen of our tune.
The rhythm is a straight 1 2 3 4.

Try the bar for yourself:
   1 2 3 4   "NE--VER GET TO.."

So, let's move on to the second bar,
Bar Fourteen of our tune.

Again, the rhythm is a straight
1 2 3 4.

This time the chord changes in the
middle of the bar, a change from
G7 to F.

Now, on Count Three the thumb rock
is marked on the sixth string held
down behind the first fret.

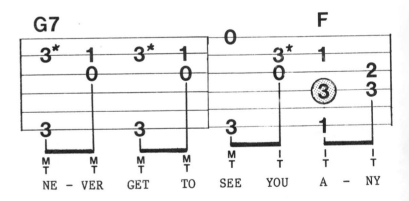

NE - VER   GET   TO   SEE   YOU   A - NY

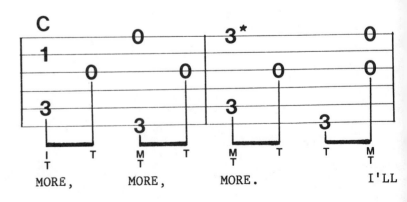

MORE,   MORE,   MORE.   I'LL

How can that be? We don't play the sixth string in an F chord.

Well, what note would we get if we held down the sixth string behind the first fret?

The sixth string is E—so a half tone higher would be F. So it would make sense to play a bass rock F note in an F chord—but how?

Look at this.

F MAJOR

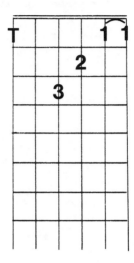

It's our F chord fingering, but now I've marked the sixth string held down behind the first fret—with your thumb.

If you find it impossible—on a classical-width fingerboard, for instance—use the note I've marked in the shaded circle. A thumb pick on the fourth string held down behind the third fret.

I'll take you through the bar.

Hold down a G7 chord.

Count One. The thumb picks the sixth string held down behind the third fret by your G7 chord. At the same time, your middle finger picks the open fifth string. (Lift your first finger off the chord.)

Count Two. Thumb rocks over onto the open third string. At the same time, your index finger picks the second string held down behind the third fret by your pinky. (Remember the asterisk!)

Change to an F chord.
Can you get your thumb around to the sixth string?
If not, use that shaded note.

Count Three. Thumb picks the sixth string held behind the first fret. At the same time, the index finger picks the second string held behind the first fret by your F chord.

Count Four. Thumb rocks over onto the fourth string held down behind the third fret by your F chord. At the same time, the index finger picks the third string held down—also by the chord—behind the second fret.

Here's the bar: 1 2 3 4   "SEE YOU A-NY"

Not too difficult, I hope.

Right. Moving on, let's look at the third bar, Bar Fifteen of our tune.

We have a chord change to C and the rhythm is a straight 1 2 3 4.

Try it. Here's the bar: 1 2 3 4   "MORE...MORE"

The last bar, Bar Sixteen of our tune, is just as easy—as are the remaining bars of the tune.

So, go back to the intro bar and play the whole tune right through to the end.

A Scale in G Major

It always surprises me that people expect scales to be boring. Nothing could be further from the truth. Scales are the building blocks of music and they can unlock the fingerboard and allow you to play the whole instrument. The thing to realize is that scales are EASY to learn--and to play. The only time they can get tedious is if you're forced to play them over and over and over and... It's not necessary to do that. Once you can play a scale, we'll use it in a tune.

So, let's unlock the fingerboard with a scale in G Major.

Now, you can pick a scale with your fingers, or by alternately picking with your thumb and index finger or you can pick it with a plectrum--or what they call in the States, a flat or straight pick.

For now, I'd like you to use a flat pick.

Hold it like this.

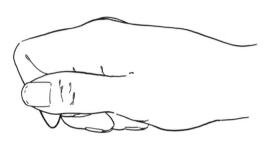

HAND & PICK DIAGRAM

Bend your index finger, place the pick on it...and hold it with your thumb.

Don't hold it too firmly or your playing will sound stiff. Just exert enough pressure so that the pick doesn't slide. It's better to drop your pick occasionally than develop a cramped right hand by holding the pick too tightly. EVERYONE drops picks--even the great players keep a couple of spares within easy reach.

Right, here's your first scale. G Major.

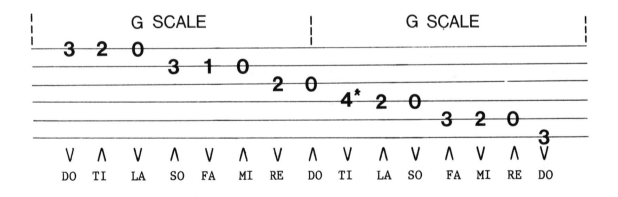

I've marked pick movements under each note. V is a down-pick, while ∧ is an up-pick.

Try the scale, remembering to pick down, up, down, up etc., exactly the way I've marked it.

As you can see, we can actually play two scales without moving out of the first playing position. Start at the high DO on the first string and play, SLOWLY, down through the DO on the open third string--to the low DO on the sixth.

Don't be in a hurry. Learn to finger it smoothly and you'll find that the speed will come without your forcing it. Concentrate on playing it RIGHT.

Also, make sure that you use your pinky for that TI on the fourth string.

O.K. Now, let's pick the scale going upward--starting at the low DO on the sixth string and playing through to the high DO on the first string.

Not so difficult, is it?

How about another scale.

A Scale in C Major

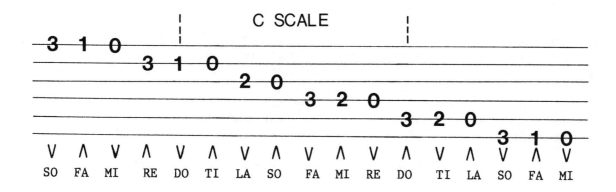

As you can see, here we have only ONE complete scale, with some extra notes at either end.

Start picking on the DO at the first fret of the second string and take it all the way down to the low DO on the fifth string.

How did you get on?

O.K. Try playing back UP to the DO on the second string.

Play up and down the scale to get your fingers used to the movements.

Right, try it from the DO on the second string right down to MI on the sixth.

Some players, like George Van Epps, have had special guitars built with a SEVENTH string and they can play the RE and DO, getting the whole lower scale--but we normal mortals have to make do with a lower scale that bottoms out on MI.

If we can't complete the lower scale, however, how about completing the fragment that occurs ABOVE the scale?

Start at the DO on the fifth string and play up to the DO on the second string...then keep on going...RE MI FA SO.

Now look at this.

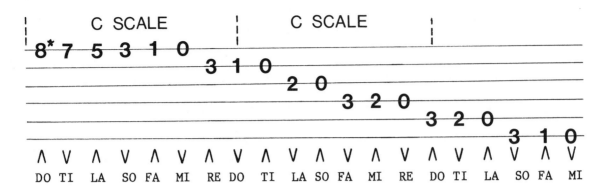

Here are the missing notes: LA, TI and DO.

They are played at the FIFTH POSITION on the fingerboard.

Fingerboard positions get their names from where the first finger falls. For example, if you hold down a chord up the fingerboard and your first finger is behind the seventh fret--you're in seventh position. In the case of this C scale, the last three notes are played in FIFTH position--so your first finger will play behind the fifth fret, you second finger will play behind the sixth fret, your third finger behind the seventh fret and your pinky behind the eighth fret.

So, start your scale at the DO on the second string and come up to the SO on the first string.

     DO RE MI FA SO

Now move your hand to the fifth position--and complete the scale.

     LA TI DO

Practice

Practice "My Home's Across the Blue Ridge Mountains."

Play over both the G and C scales until you can play them without looking at the tab.

UNLOCKING THE FINGERBOARD

If you have practiced the scales you should find that they are speeding up without your having to force it. It happens naturally when your left and right hands begin to develop coordination.

I think it's time to show you how to unlock the fingerboard.

Let's consider your G scale.

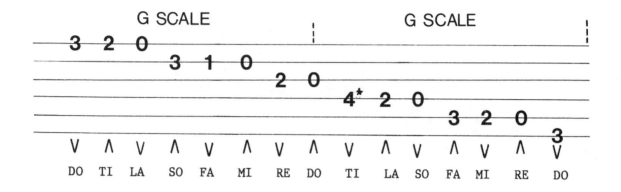

If I put a capo on the fingerboard just behind the first fret--what key would that scale fingering actually produce?

A♭ --or to give the key its other name, G#.

And...if I put the capo on behind the second fret--and played the G scale fingering--I'd actually be playing a scale in the key of A.

So, by using the capo I could, if I wanted, play a scale in A♭, A, B♭, B, C, C#, D, E♭, E.....It would be rather awkward to move a capo any higher on the fingerboard--but you can see that just one scale fingering can let you play in up to NINE different keys--just by moving the capo!

So, what actually does a capo do?

It frets strings on the fingerboard, just as a finger does.

But if it's just like a finger--why don't we just USE a finger? That way we don't need a capo--and we can use the whole fingerboard--even the piece right over the soundboard.

It's simple. All we have to do is this.

Everywhere your scale shows an open string--in other words, everywhere a note would be played by the capo, we must use the first finger.

Look.

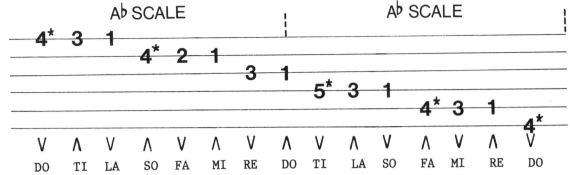

It's a G scale--but written out one fret higher, making it an A♭ (or if you prefer, a G♯) scale.

Everywhere I had an open string before, I now have a fretted string--and the finger I use to fret those notes is the first finger.

Try the new fingering.

    DO TI LA SO FA MI RE DO TI LA SO FA MI RE DO.

How did you get on? You're having to use your pinky a lot more in this new fingering, which is why I got you strengthening it a while back.

O.K. Try coming UP the scale.

    DO RE MI FA SO LA TI DO RE MI FA SO LA TI DO.

Now look at this.

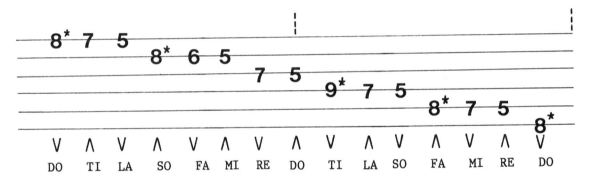

Same scale fingering, different position on the board.

Try it. Start with your pinky on the first string behind the eighth fret.

    DO TI LA SO FA MI RE DO TI LA SO FA MI RE DO.

Come back up.

    DO RE MI FA SO LA TI DO RE MI FA SO LA TI DO.

Good! What key was that, by the way?

Your DO is always the key note--so...

    G A♭ A B♭ B C

That was a scale of C Major.

Now we already know a scale of C Major--and, in fact, we borrowed three notes from the scale which you just played...

LA TI DO

...to complete the C scale that I showed you in Lesson Eight.

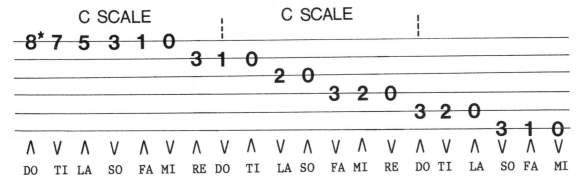

So you now have TWO ways in which you can play a scale, or a melody, in the key of C.

        1. Using a G scale fingering at the fifth position.
        2. Using a C scale fingering at the first position.

You can even combine them, like this.

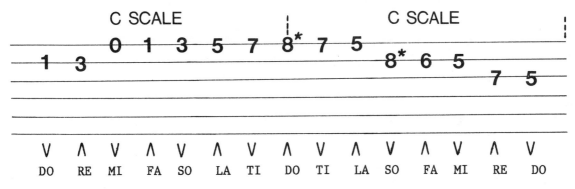

Not so difficult, is it?

Now, in the same way that we can play our G scale fingering anywhere on the fingerboard to give us a wide range of keys, we can also move the C scale.

If we played it as if we had a capo on at the first fret--the scale would actually be a C# scale.

If we played it as if the capo were on at the second fret--the scale would be in D.

How about if we put our imaginary capo on behind the seventh fret? In what key would our scale be?

                C C# D Eb E F F#...G

We'd have a G scale.
Try it.

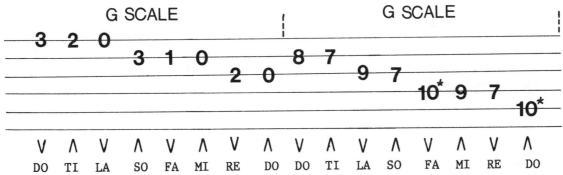

61

What I'd like you to do is take some time to experiment with these two fingerings. You'll find that they'll take you all over the board. Every good guitar player that I know spends some time during every rehearsal running these two scale fingerings all over the board. They call it "noodling." Just think of a simple tune and see in how many places you can play it. Don't make it work, make it FUN!

Here's a country rock tune that came to me the other evening while I was "noodling" on a new electric guitar I'd just received from Tony Zemaitis. Tony and I go back almost thirty years so you can imagine that I couldn't wait to get my fingers on the guitar. I call the tune "Take Your Pick."

TAKE YOUR PICK

John Pearse

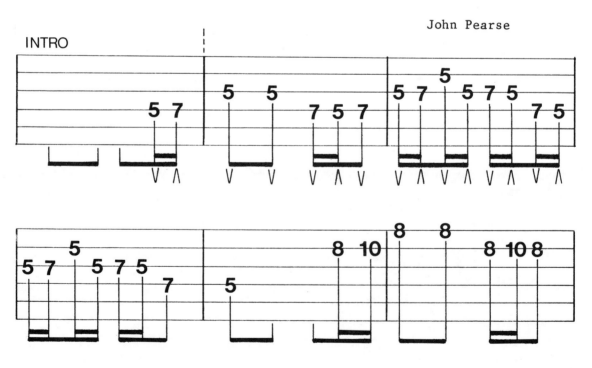

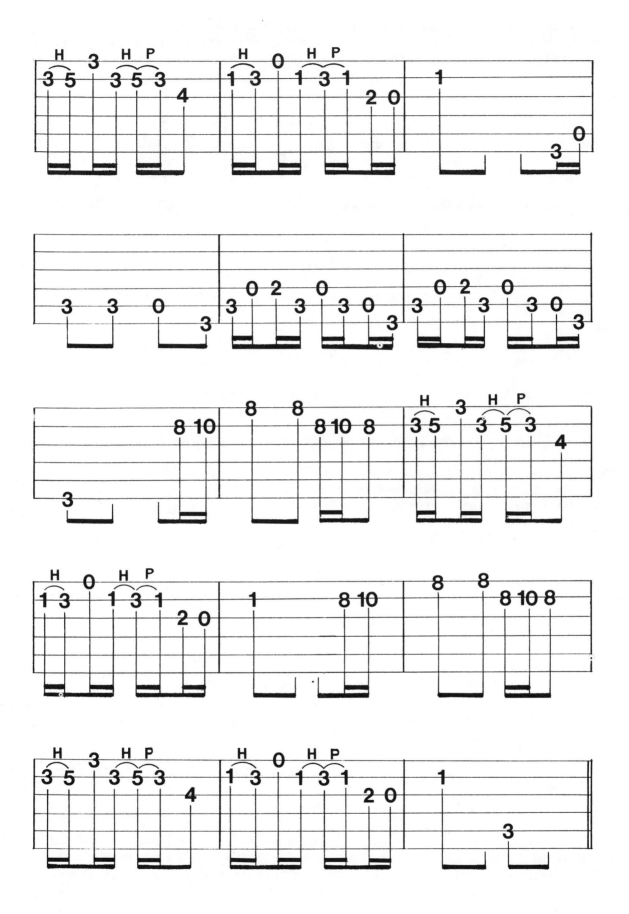

The tune is in 4/4.

Let's look at the intro bar and the first two bars. You'll notice that everything is played out of the fifth fret. The logical finger to use there is the first finger--so this sequence is in fifth position.

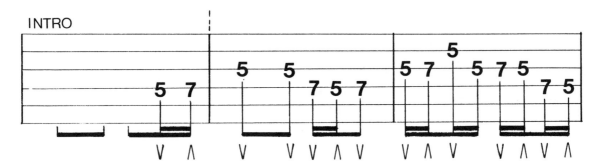

The rhythm of the Intro is 1 2 3 4& with Counts One, Two and Three silent.

Count Four. First finger holds down the fourth string just behind the fifth fret.

"And" Count. Third finger holds down the fourth string just behind the seventh fret.

The rhythm of Bar One is 1 2 3& 4. Play fifth fret notes with your first finger and seventh fret notes with your third finger.

The same goes for Bar Two, the rhythm of which is 1& 2& 3& 4&.

When you get to Bar Four you'll find that the position switches from fifth to eighth position, bringing the first finger up to its new base at the eighth fret.

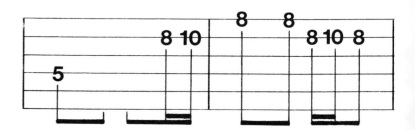

In Bars Six and Seven...

...we encounter both hammer on and pull off movements.

Let's look at Bar Six.

The picking sequence is based at the third fret so we can assume it will be easiest to play it in third position--with the first finger at the third fret.

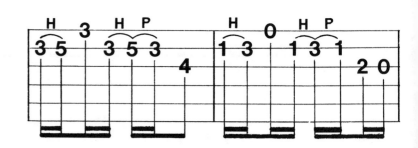

Since many of the notes are played at the same fret on neighboring strings, it would probably be a good idea to use your first finger to fret both the first and the second strings at the third fret. (This is the way it frets those strings in an F chord. We call this fingering a "barre.")

Bar Seven is a very similar picking sequence--but here played out of first position.

In Bar Eight...

...we start a restatement of
the melody in a lower octave...

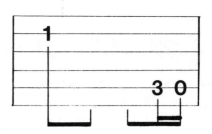

...which takes us through to
Bar Twelve...

...which begins the first of
two four bar repeats which end
the tune.

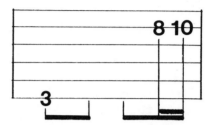

Like many country rock solos, this is not complex to play. Its effect relies
upon subtleties that YOU can bring out in your playing. Experiment with the
phrasing and the force with which you pick the strings. Above all, the solo
should sound as smooth as possible--and still pop along!

Practice ─────────────────────────

"Noodle" your G and C scales. In particular, practice starting a scale in one
fingering and completing it in the other.

Practice "Take Your Pick" until you feel you are beginning to put some of your
own ideas into it.

10 COUNTRY FLAT PICKING

In the tune in Lesson Nine, we were using the flat pick to play a very flowing melodic line--rather like a horn solo. In fact, many rock and jazz guitar players get their inspiration from listening to recordings of such great jazz horn players as Charlie Parker and Bix Beiderbecke. I've often been influenced by keyboard players, too. Players like Louis Van Dyke, for example, or, on synthesizer, Jan Hammer...both of whom play music that translates perfectly to the guitar. You should listen to as much non-guitar music as possible. You'll be surprised what you might pick up!

In the United States, the flat pick is used not only as a means of playing a fluid melodic line, it also fills in a suggestion of backup behind a melody--or just strums a backup alone with maybe the occasional melodic run at the end of a line.

Hold your flat pick as I showed you in the last lesson. Now, do you remember how we played the 4/4 Carter style variation?

Remember you picked with the thumb, then your index finger grazed up, then down and then up again.

Well, a great deal of country flat-picking is developed from that simple finger style. Look at this.

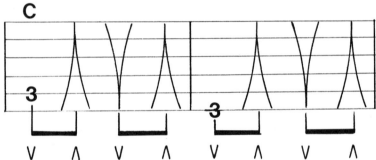

It's your 4/4 Carter style variation but played with a flat pick.
Try it.

Now, look how this down-pick, up-pick, down-pick, up-pick movement can be used to play a melodic line.

Instead of an up-strum or down-strum, we can up-pick or down-pick a note.

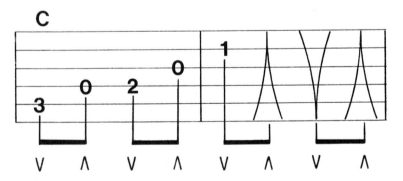

Often a country player will pick a very intricate intro for a song and then just use a simple 4/4 pick to provide a backup to the voice. Like this:

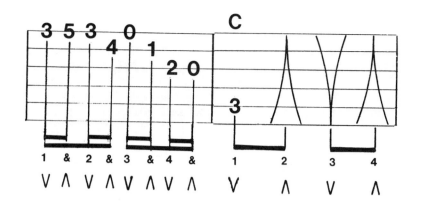

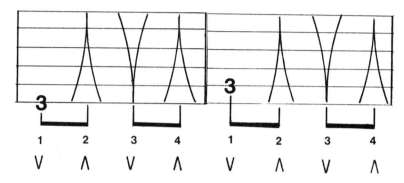

But, whatever he or she picks, the flow of the accompaniment will be uninterrupted.

Now, many pickers don't try flat-picking a tune in waltz time because they think the flow is more difficult to keep going.

I enjoy flat-picking waltzes and you will too, if you'll just spend a few minutes on this next TAB example.

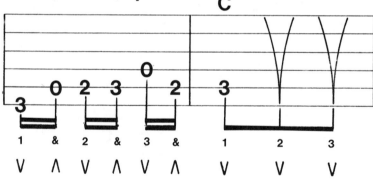

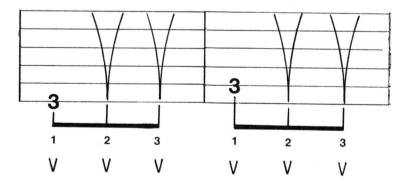

You can see that it really isn't difficult to integrate an up, down, up melody line with a down, down, down accompaniment, is it?

Here's one of my favorite country waltzes, "The Storms Are on the Ocean."

THE STORMS ARE ON THE OCEAN

Trad. arr. J. Pearse

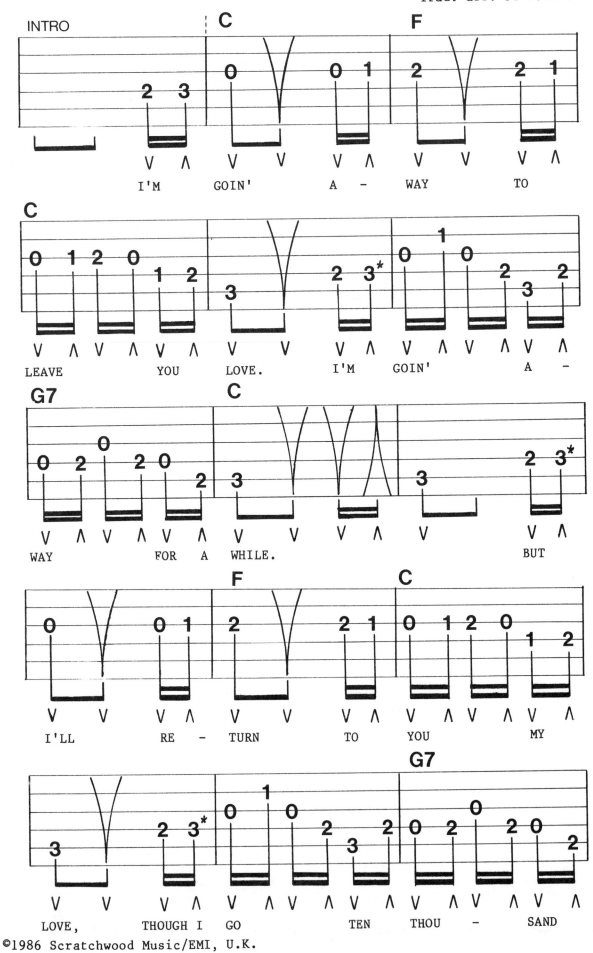

68

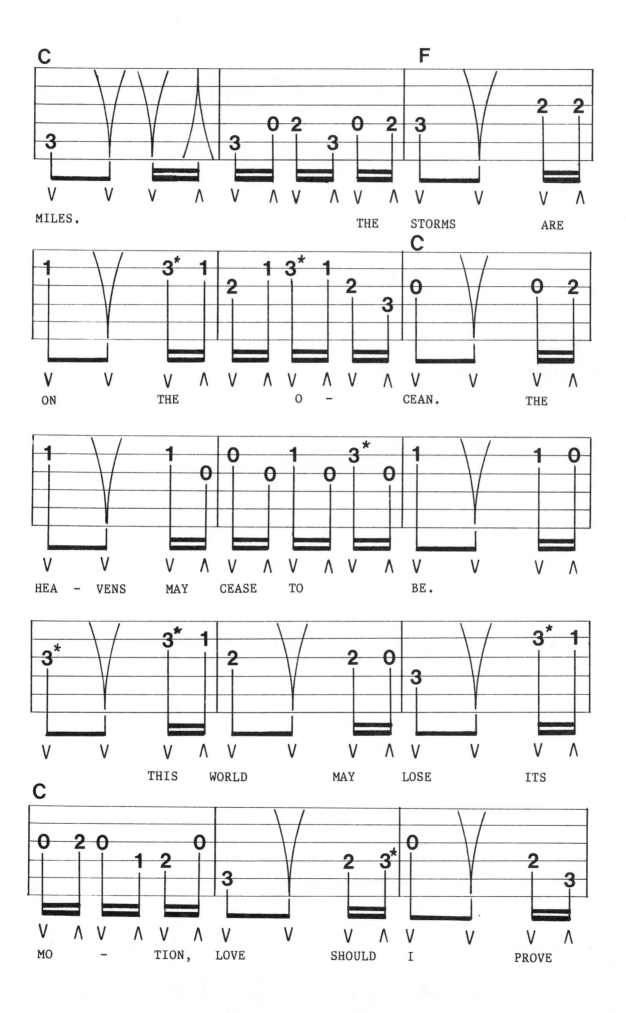

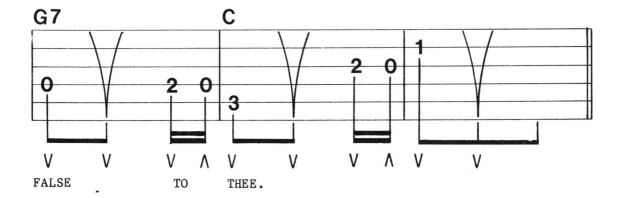

FALSE . TO THEE.

2. Oh, who will shoe your pretty foot
   And who will glove your hand?
   And who will kiss your ruby lips
   While I'm in a far off land?
        Cho: The storms etc.

3. Oh, Papa will shoe my pretty foot
   And Mama will glove my hand.
   And sister will kiss my ruby lips
   While you're in a far off land.
        Cho: The storms etc.

4. There's many a change in the stars above
   And change in the clouds design.
   There's many a change in a young man's heart
   But there's never a change in mine.
        Cho: The storms etc.

5. Oh, there's many a star burns in the West
   That falls like a flake of snow.
   And there's many a damn on a cruel young man
   That would treat a poor girl so.
        Cho: The storms etc.

Take it slowly and you shouldn't have any difficulty.

Here are just a few tips to help you.

Intro Bar. The rhythm is 1 2 3&, with Counts One and Two silent.

Bars Three, Five, Six, Eleven, Thirteen, Fourteen, Sixteen, Nineteen,
Twenty-two and Twenty-seven are all 1& 2& 3&.

Good luck.

Practice _____

Work out some intro melodies and practice going from them into both 4/4 and 3/4
accompaniment strums.

Practice "The Storms are on the Ocean," concentrating on keeping the 3/4 rhythm
steady.

70

THE CLASSICAL GUITAR

Before we tackle some classical guitar technique it might be a good idea if you turn back to the section on holding the guitar, just to make sure that you remember the correct classical position. By now you should not be quite so dependent upon seeing the fingerboard when you play as you were just a few weeks back, but if you are--don't worry. Just don't bend your back and crane over to look at the frets. Most guitars have small position marks along the side of the fingerboard that should be clearly visible even if you're sitting in a straight backed classical position. If your guitar doesn't have such marks, you can do what Chet Atkins does. He sticks a small piece of adhesive tape on the BACK of the neck to act as a reference point while he's playing. I must admit to doing that myself on the odd occasions when I have to play a guitar without position marks.

By the way, are you using a thumb pick? Orthodox classical players tend to frown on the use of thumb picks--although one of the finest, Mario Macafferi, always played with one--and Chet Atkins invariably uses a thumb pick whenever he plays classical guitar. I'd try it without if you can. Remember to keep your thumb straight and out well in front of your fingers.

Left Hand Vibrato

If, when you pick a string, you rock your fretting finger to and fro along the axis of the string, you will produce a left-hand vibrato.

What it actually does is minutely raise and lower the pitch of the vibrating string, setting up a wave form...

...that both prolongs the note and intensifies it. To better understand what I mean, get someone to stand across the room from you and sing, very quietly, "AAAAAAAAAAAAAH." Next, get them to sing, at the same quiet level,"YA YA YA YA YA YA YA YA." You will find that the second example will be much more audible because it has now been overlaid by a wave form.

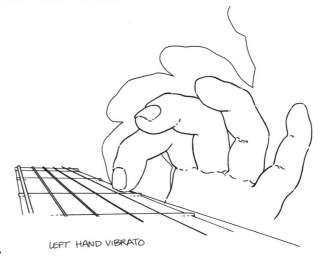

LEFT HAND VIBRATO

Rock and blues guitarists also use left-hand vibrato, but one in which they alternately pull and push a vibrating string sideways, sawing it across a fret. The overlaid wave form produced in this way is very crude but can be effective in certain types of tunes. The sawing motion, however, is bad for strings and very hard on frets.

Right, let's move along to our tune--a piece I wrote after having produced an album by the fine classical guitarist David Tannenbaum. I call it "Spring Solstice."

Play it A A B A. Part A twice, Part B once, and finish by playing Part A once again.

SPRING SOLSTICE

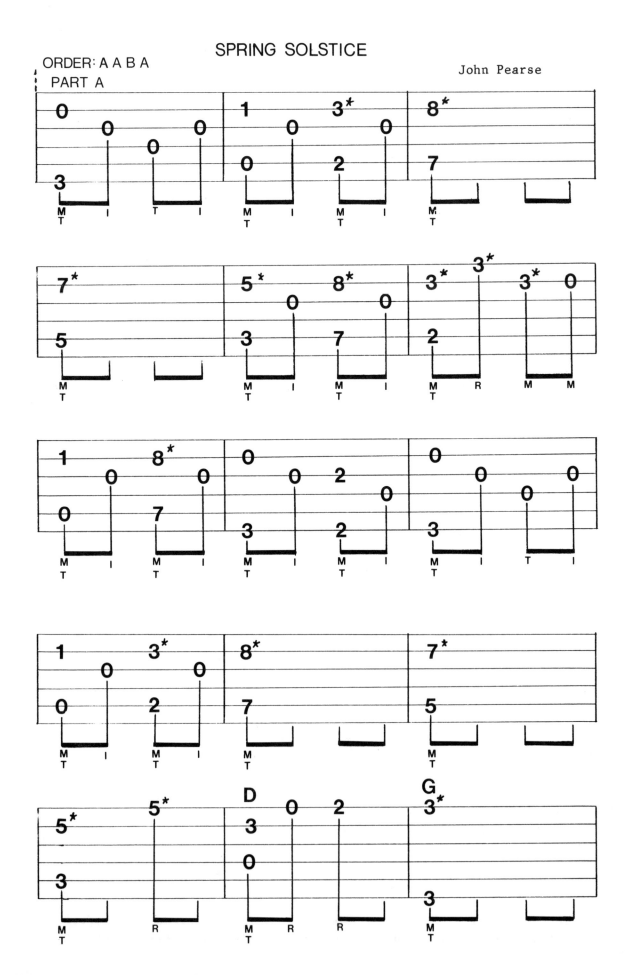

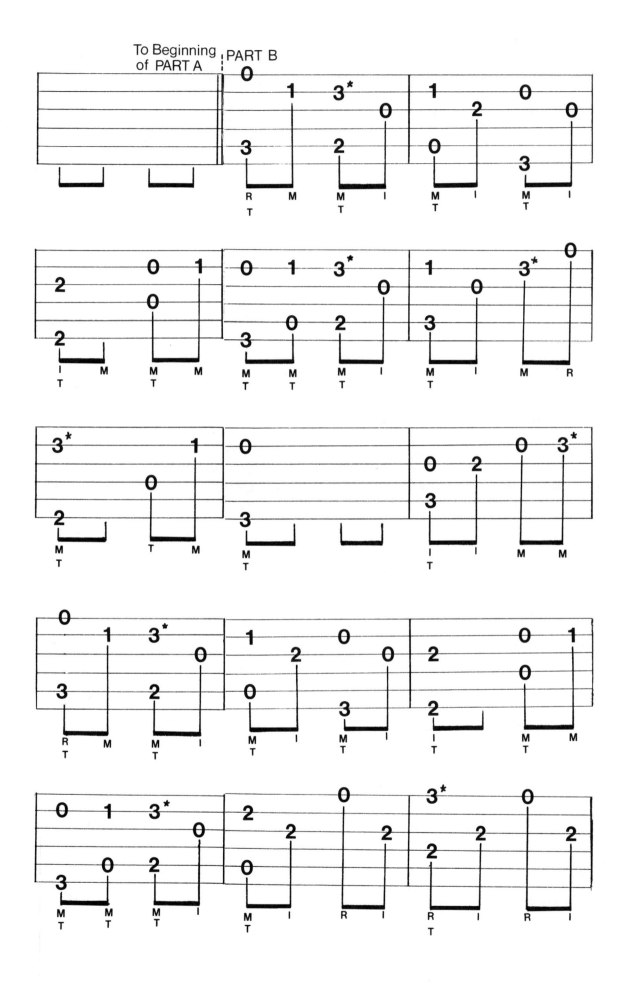

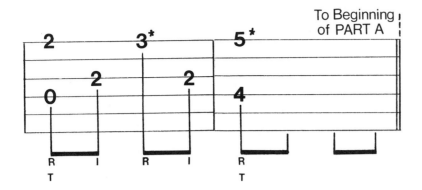

How did you get on?

All the bars are pretty straightforward without any awkward
rhythms, but some of your left hand travels, especially in
Bar Seven might take a little getting used to.

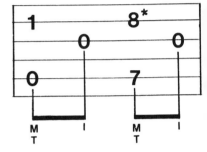

The pinky really comes into its full glory in this tune as it
carries a great deal of the melody. If you have been putting
in at least fifteen minutes a day--every day--on your guitar,
you should have no difficulty in playing the piece. If your
pinky does rebel, however, take breaks every few minutes but don't be tempted
to switch to another finger. You should use the pinky.

Practice

Really spend time on "Spring Solstice" because, like "Take Your Pick," it is a
deceptively easy sounding--and playing--piece. Concentrate not only on getting
the right notes, but also on getting a GOOD TONE.

Experiment with moving your right hand close to--or further away--from the
bridge to vary the QUALITY of the notes that you are playing. The closer to the
bridge, the more "brittle" the tone--the farther away, the warmer and "darker"
the sound. Playing the right notes is only fifty percent of being a good
guitarist--the other fifty percent is playing them in such a way that people
will want to listen.

12 A NEW TUNING

In this lesson we're going to learn a new tuning and a new way to play the guitar. Up until now we have been using the standard Spanish tuning, namely E A D G B E. Now we'll be putting our guitars into a tuning called Open G. Before we do, however, you will have to get a Hawaiian nut adapter from your local music store.

This is a little metal gizmo that fits neatly over the top nut of your guitar to raise the strings high enough from the fingerboard that they won't rattle against the frets when you're playing with a metal slide bar.

HAWAIIAN NUT ADAPTER

You just loosen the strings, slide the adapter under them and over the nut, then tune your strings again.

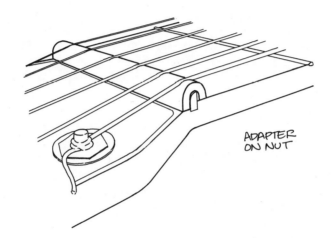

ADAPTER ON NUT

There are many different kinds of slide bars, from the massive bullet shaped bars used by pedal steel players to the little flat traditional Hawaiian bars, but the best one for our purposes is the easy-to-hold Stevens bar. Like the nut adapter, the Stevens bar is easily obtained through your local music store, though they may have to order it specially.

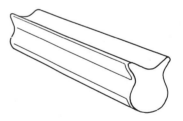

STEVENS BAR

Open G Tuning

In Standard Tuning it is necessary to hold down certain strings in order to make a chord. In our new tuning, the strings are tuned in such a way that fingering is not necessary. When played open, the strings play a chord of G, hence the name "Open G Tuning."

As you should know by now, the notes of a G chord are G, B and D--so we have to retune each string of the guitar to one of those notes.

Put your nut adapter over the nut and let's begin.

Our Standard Tuning is E A D G B E, so we can leave the second, third and fourth strings alone--and just change the tuning on the first, fifth and sixth strings.

This is what we do.

We drop the first string DOWN ONE TONE, from E to D.

We raise the fifth string UP ONE TONE, from A to B.

We raise the sixth string UP ONE AND ONE-HALF TONES, from E to G.

Our tuning is now G B D G B D.

It's not a good idea to keep switching between slide and standard configurations on your guitar as the different tensions of the two can weaken the neck. For now it's O.K., but if you fall in love with this way of playing, I'd recommend you look out for another guitar that you can leave set up like this permanently--you'd be surprised how good a ratty old yard sale $10 special can sound when it's played with a slide. If you really get serious about the style, you might consider getting a guitar specifically built for slide playing with an especially high top nut. A guitar built like this is called a Hawaiian style guitar. The one that immediately comes to mind is the Dobro which was invented back in the twenties by two Czechoslovakian immigrants, the Dopyera Brothers (DO-BRO), who were looking for a way to amplify the sound of a Hawaiian-style guitar mechanically. They came up with a system involving an aluminum resonator which gave the guitar its characteristic keening sound. Folks either love the Dobro--or hate it. I love it--and in addition to owning a number of beautiful new Dobros, I haunt pawn shops in search of battered survivors from the thirties and forties.

Pawn shops are a good place to find normal Hawaiian style guitars, also. There was a real boom in Hawaiian music in the twenties, and millions of Hawaiian style guitars were both imported from Hawaii and built here in the States. My favorite "real" Hawaiian guitar is a Kona (you sometimes see them marked "Weissenborn, Los Angeles," but these were apparently made in Hawaii by Kona and sold through the Weissenborn chain on the mainland) because they have a particularly rich sound in the bass range. Listen to David Lindley on old Jackson Browne recordings--that acoustic slide guitar is a Weissenborn-Kona. Other companies that made good Hawaiian-style guitars were C.F. Martin (their koawood 0-18s and 0-28s keep popping up in pawn shops--lovely guitars--and you may be lucky enough to come across a pearl-inlaid 00-40H!) and Gibson.

Be on the lookout, also, for Electric Hawaiian-style guitars. These are called "lap steels" and are the forerunners of today's pedal steel guitar. Like the acoustic Hawaiian-style guitars, nobody seems to want them today, and you can often pick them up for a song. Don't be put off by garish plastic pearloid and chrome. Plastic was very new back then and players preferred state-of-the-art real plastic over old fashioned mother-of-pearl! I once had an extremely garish Teisco lap steel that was encrusted with genuine "mother-of-barstool" plastic. I hated to look at it--but, boy what a sound it had!
Again, listen to Lindley. He often plays
a Teisco lap steel on his records.

Holding the Steel
Place the steel along the edge of your
second finger, rest your first finger
along the top, and hold the steel snugly
against your second finger by pressure
of your thumb.

Your remaining fingers--the third and your
pinky--rest on the strings BEHIND the bar to
muffle them and prevent them from ringing.

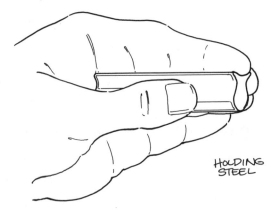

HOLDING STEEL

The bar may feel a little awkward at first, so carry it around in your pocket for a few days and get used to the feel of it in your hand.

Right, now that we're in Open G and we know how to hold the bar...what next?

Well, if our open strings give us the chord of G... where would our C chord be?

G open, A♭, A, B♭, B....C. Fifth fret!

So, if we rest the bar over the fifth fret (OVER it, not behind it) we will get a chord of C. Try it.

What about D7? Remember, because of our tuning, it's awkward to get a seventh, but how about a D? We can use that instead. Well, if the fifth fret gives us a C chord...the next fret will give us a C# and next to that, the seventh fret, will give us a D.

So open gives us G. Fifth fret gives us a C and seventh fret gives us D. Try it for yourself. Make sure you're right over the fret. Don't push down, just rest the bar and let your third finger and pinky trail behind it to muffle the strings between your bar and the headstock end of the neck.

So, what happens if we come up to the twelfth fret?

Right, we get another G chord, the OCTAVE of the open chord.

So, if the twelfth fret gives us a G...

...five frets HIGHER will give us another C...

...and two frets up from that will give us another D.
Simple isn't it.

How about if you wanted to play a tune in the key of D?

Where is D?

Right, at the seventh fret. So to find our Basic Chord Sequence we count from this fret.

Where is G?

Five frets up from the D, at the twelfth fret.

How about A? (Remember we can't get the seventh easily.)

Seven frets up from the D, in other words, at the fourteenth fret.

So, using this simple procedure of locating the key chord and then counting up five frets or seven frets you can get the Basic Chord Sequence in any key. Experiment for yourself.

Of course, in the key of D, for instance, we could also have played a G chord by playing the strings open, couldn't we?

How about an A?

Right, we could have rested the bar over the SECOND fret.

G open, A♭ at the first fret, A at the second fret.

Playing a Scale

In Open G most notes of the major scale follow a very easy to remember bar pattern...

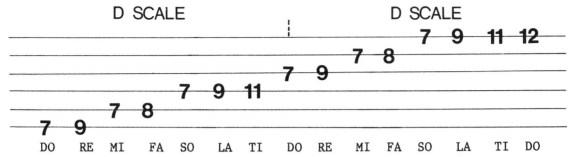

...which can be moved up or down the fingerboard in order to play in any key.

If, however, you are playing a tune that contains harmonies or in which you must include chords, then your scale pattern may have to be abandoned to allow you to play certain melody notes that need either a harmony or a chord backing at a fret where a needed chord is located.

Like this.

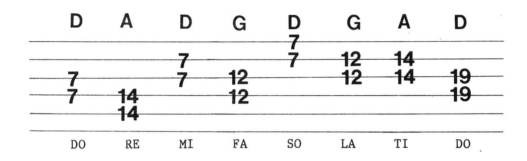

As a general rule, although following the bar pattern is easy, it's not a good idea to play just single string melodies. You should always try to take advantage of the great harmonies that are so much a part of slide guitar. Work out a tune in the basic bar pattern to start off, but then look for harmonies and chords that you can add to flesh out the arrangement and make it more interesting.

How about a tune?

Here is one I wrote some years ago when I taught guitar to a girl who had just returned from a scientific expedition on Easter Island. She told me that the Islanders' name for their island was Rapanui and I thought it was such a lovely name that I wrote a tune for it.

RAPANUI

John Pearse

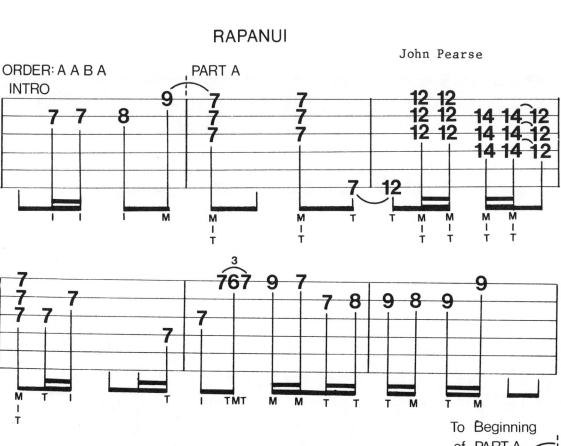

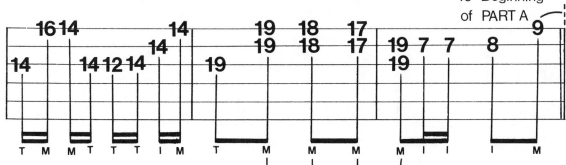

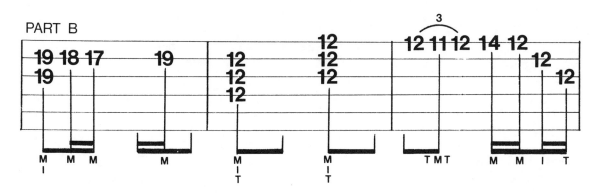

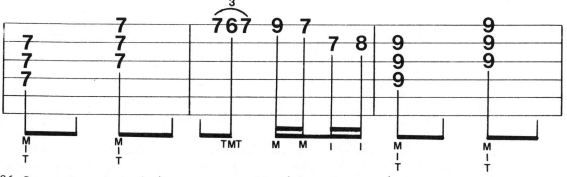

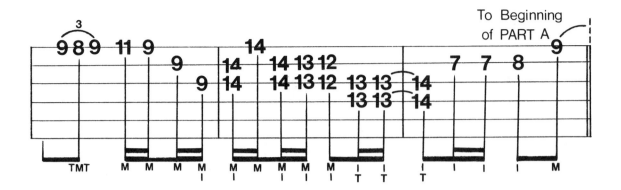

The tune is in 4/4 and shouldn't give you much trouble, if you take it slowly!

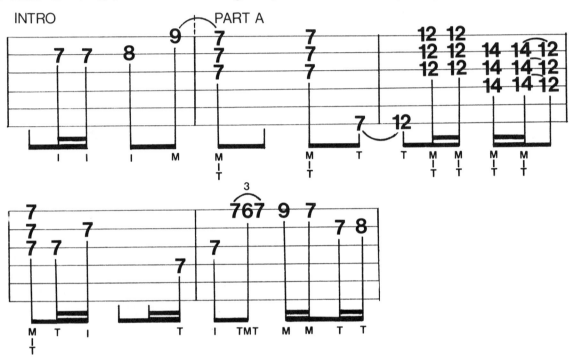

Intro Bar. The rhythm is 1 2& 3 4, with Count One silent. On Count Four, you'll see a bow linking it to Count One of the next bar. This means you should SLIDE your bar from the ninth fret, first string, to the seventh fret.

We don't want any other strings involved in the slide, so you should tilt the bar...

...using just the last half-inch or so, so that you don't get other strings that you don't want chiming in.

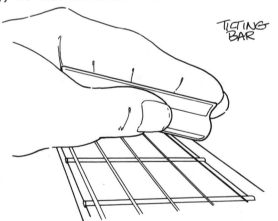

TILTING BAR

There's another slide at the end of Bar One, this time on your sixth string.

At the end of Bar Two you have a slide on three strings--the second, third and fourth--from the fourteenth to the twelfth fret. Naturally, for this slide you would not tilt the bar. By the way, the rhythm of that bar is 1 2& 3& 4.

80

When you're playing, if a slide isn't marked, don't slide from fret to fret.
Lift your bar slightly away from the strings and move to your new fret position, trailing your third finger and pinky as you go to dampen the strings.

When you get to your new fret position, rest your bar down and play.

One of the reasons why Hawaiian slide playing passed out of favor was that so
many guitarists played it badly! If every move is played as a slide the music
sounds really hokey. If, however, you use the slide as an effect, the sound can
be quite magical.

A word here, too, about bar vibrato. Many of the old players slid the bar back
and forth above the fret to get a vibrato--sometimes moving as much as half an
inch on either side of the fret. The effect was rather eye crossing, like a mix
between the singing of an alcoholic soprano and an amorous cat. If you want to
be traditional and slide the bar,
don't move it more than a half-inch
TOTAL. A better, more subtle vibrato
can be obtained by just ROCKING the
bar smoothly from side to side.

O.K. In Bar Four the rhythm is 1 2& 3& 4 and you have a triplet on Count Two.
That just means you must play THREE notes in the space of one. Now, although
there is a bow linking the notes, you don't play them as a continuous slide.
You must play so that the bar is over each marked fret BEFORE you play it. It's
not EEOOEE. It's EE OO EE--but FAST! Tilt your bar so that the other strings
don't chime in.

Look at Bars Six, Seven and Eight.

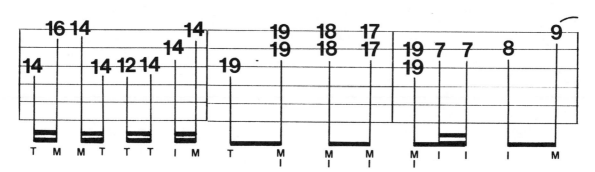

These three bars contain one of my favorite Hawaiian music clichés. The rhythm
is 1& 2& 3& 4& 1 2 3 4 1. After you've played the A part through twice, you
play Part B through and then finish off the tune with the A part once more.

Practice

Practice ACCURACY. Try to get right over the fret, not just close to it. If you
find you are just slightly off, a crafty bit of vibrato can sometimes hide
it--but remember what I said about alcoholic sopranos!

Damping with your trailing fingers, what pedal steel players call "blocking,"
is really important too, for clear and fast playing. Practice the cliché in
Bars Six, Seven and Eight until you can hit each note cleanly--and without any
hint of a slide between them. That's a very good blocking exercise.

...And, of course, practice the whole tune.

13 PEDAL STEEL MIMICRY

When the pedal steel was developed, a number of players of the old Hawaiian style guitar and electric lap steel attempted to imitate it. They did this by using their third finger to hook onto a string BEHIND the bar and pull it so that the pitch rose a half--or sometimes, a whole--tone. This technique is called a "bend" and is shown on a tablature stave by means of a box with a B above it and a bow linking it to another note.

Bending is not difficult, but you will need to spend some time to perfect it.

Try this. Rest your bar across the strings, say at the seventh fret.

Pick the second string with your middle finger.

Now, while it's still ringing, hook your left-hand third finger onto the string behind the bar...

...and pull it back and also slightly upward to keep it tight against the bar--until the note rises one fret's worth (in other words, a half tone). The movement must be smooth and accurate.

This is how that bend appears in tablature.

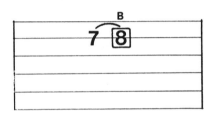

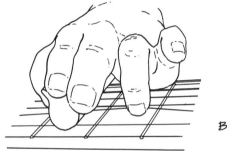

BENDING

Here's another bar containing a bend.

It comes from our new tune, which is in 3/4.
The rhythm of the bar, therefore, is 1& 2 3&.

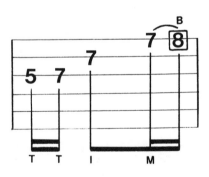

You can see that on Count Three, the first string is picked with the bar at the seventh fret AND THEN IT IS BENT TO THE VALUE OF THE FRET IN THE BOX. From the note at the seventh fret to the note that would normally be found at the eighth fret--a half tone.

In addition to bending a note upward, you can also bend it down--imitating the effect a pedal steel player gets when using a knee lever. To do this, just pick a string that has already been bent, and then relax it down to its normal pitch. This is called a REVERSE bend and is marginally more difficult because you must bend the note without being able to hear it. The only way in which you can gauge just how much the string must be pulled in order to bring it up to the starting note is to learn to recognize the pressure of the string against the pulling finger. I know that sounds impossible, but you'll be surprised how quickly your finger will learn.

Let's look at the tune. As I said a while back, it's a waltz. In fact, it's the kind of good old-fashioned country waltz that pedal steel players love to get into. Just take it really slowly until you know your way around it, and you'll soon be showing your buddies that it's not necessary to spend $3000 for a seven pedal, five-knee-lever monster that weighs seventy pounds--if you just use your guitar, a nut adapter, a bar...and a little ingenuity.

JUST AN OLD GINGHAM DRESS

John Pearse

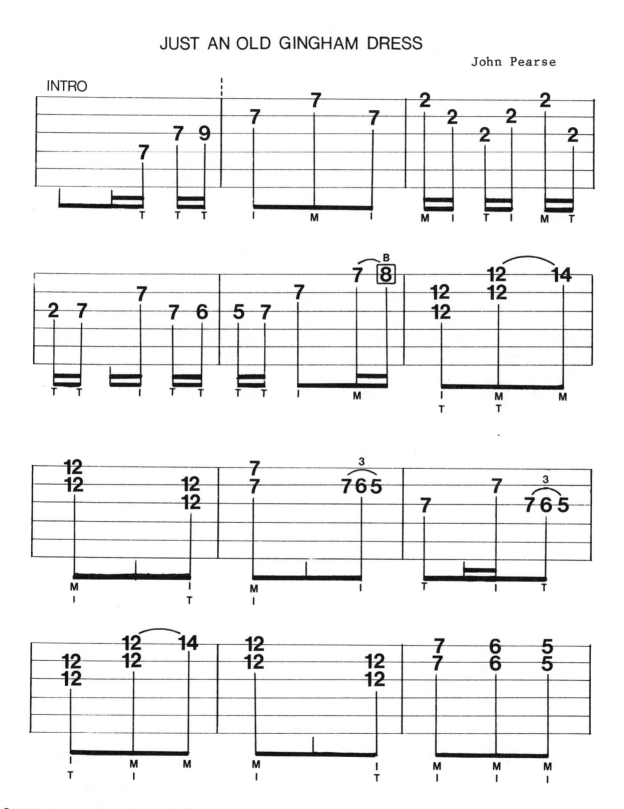

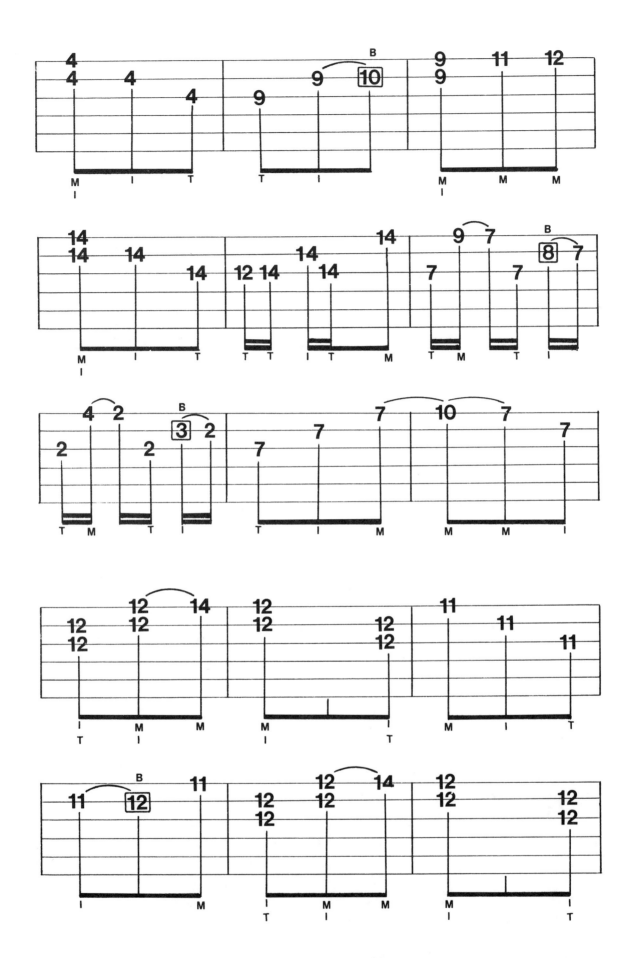

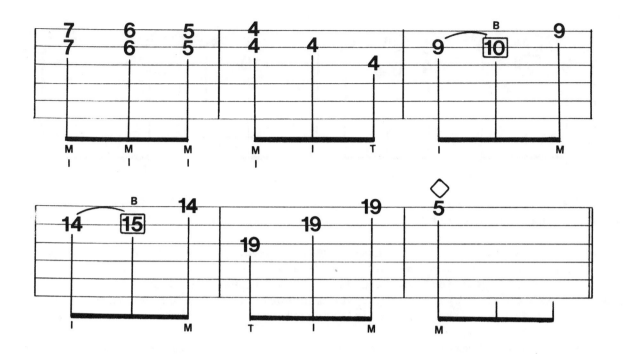

How did you get on?

You recognised Bar Four, of course!

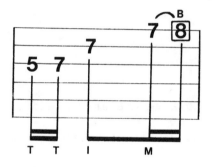

In Bars Seven and Eight there
are triplets, but they shouldn't
give you any trouble. The rhythm
of Bar Eight is 1 2& 3, by the way.

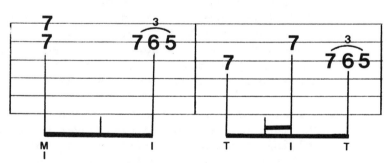

In Bars Seventeen and Eighteen,
the rhythm is 1& 2& 3&....

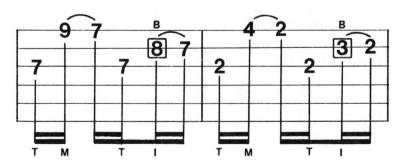

...and we have REVERSE bends as
part of a typical Buddy Emmons style
knee-lever pedal steel move. Listen
carefully to the record to make sure
that you have each emphasis right.

The last four bars of the tune...

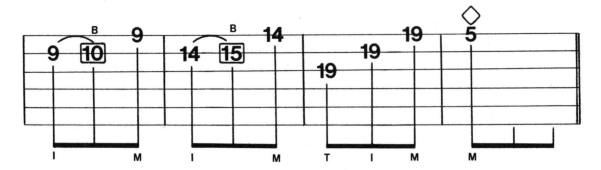

...are again typical pedal steel bars ending with a harmonic played on the first string over the fifth fret.

If you want to sound even more like a pedal steel, you can get an old electric lap steel or put a pickup on your guitar--and go electric. If you do, a good accessory to get is a foot swell pedal, which allows you to change the volume level while you're playing so that you can swell into and out of those good ol' country chords just like they do in Nashville.

Remember always, however, that no amount of expensive electrical doodads can compensate for a badly played piece--so learn it right first, then buy gadgets.

Well, here we are at the end of the first thirteen lessons.

I'm glad you stayed with me. I expect you are too.

What you should do now is go back right to the first lesson and review every-thing I've shown you. With the experience you now have, even a simple style like a Carter variation will sound richer and more exciting the second time around. You now know how to play melody--so work out some melodies using the various Carter styles, carrying the melody on the thumb, and how about trying out some flat-picking on slide guitar? Tut Taylor does it, why not you?

Segovia once called the guitar "an orchestra" because of its many voices and the many moods it can evoke. Never be afraid to experiment with new ways of holding down chords, different ways of tuning the strings, or unusual playing techniques. The guitar is going through a Renaissance these days, and many more people are developing exciting ideas on the instrument than at any other time in its long history. It's a good time to be starting out.

So enjoy!

HAPPY PLAYING!

FRETBOARD DIAGRAM

As you discovered, when I showed you how to build chords, some notes have more than one name. G#, for instance, is also known as A♭; C# is also known as D♭. Notes or keys that sound the same but have different names are said to be ENHARMONIC. Here is a fretboard diagram showing all the enharmonic equivalents

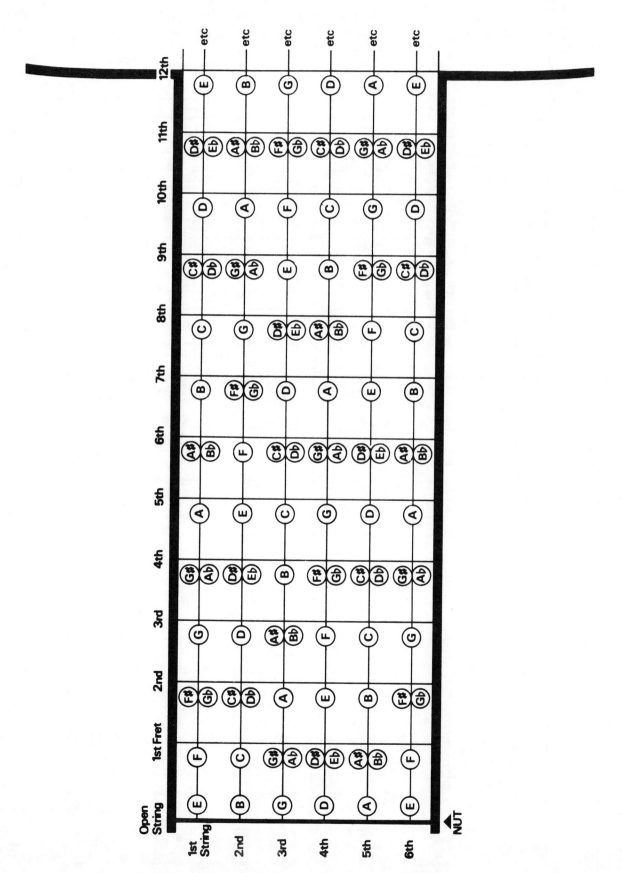

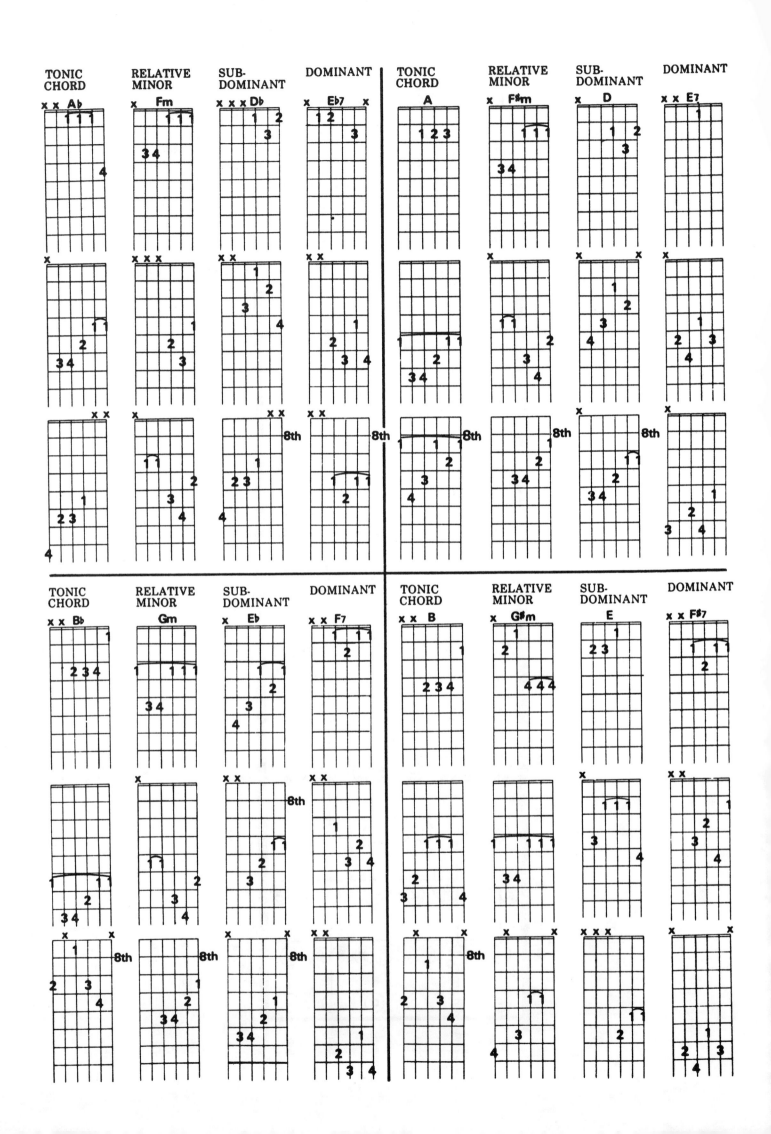

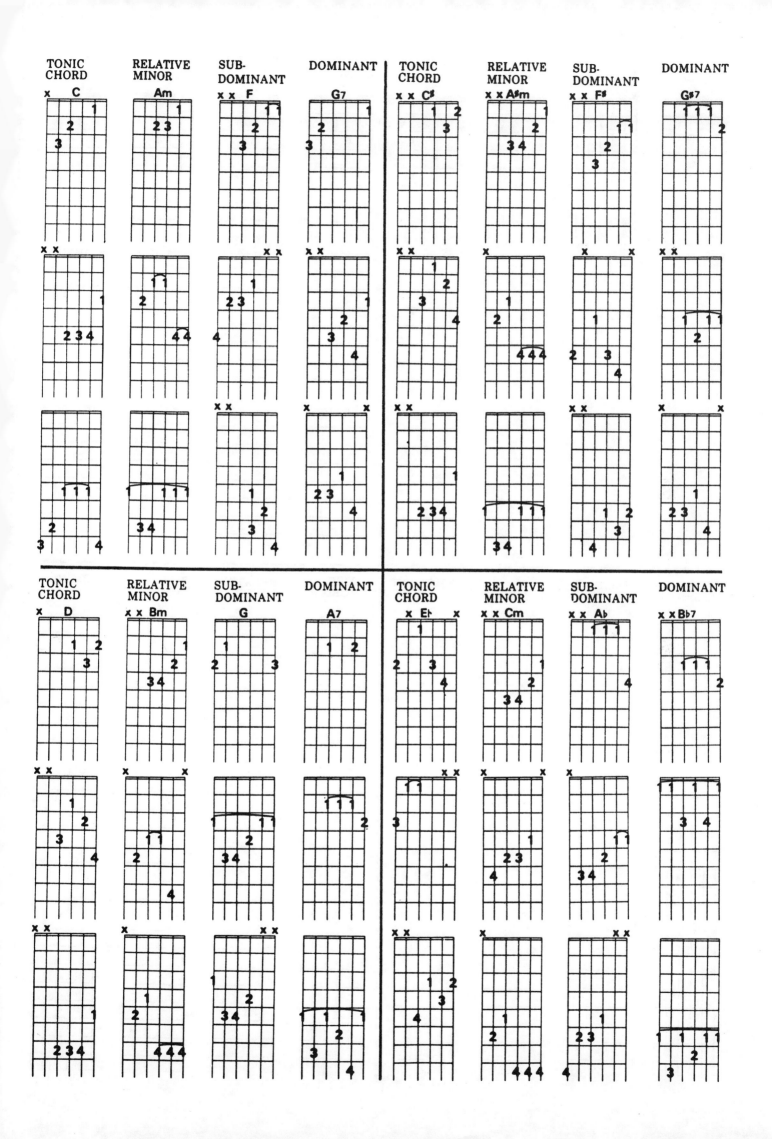

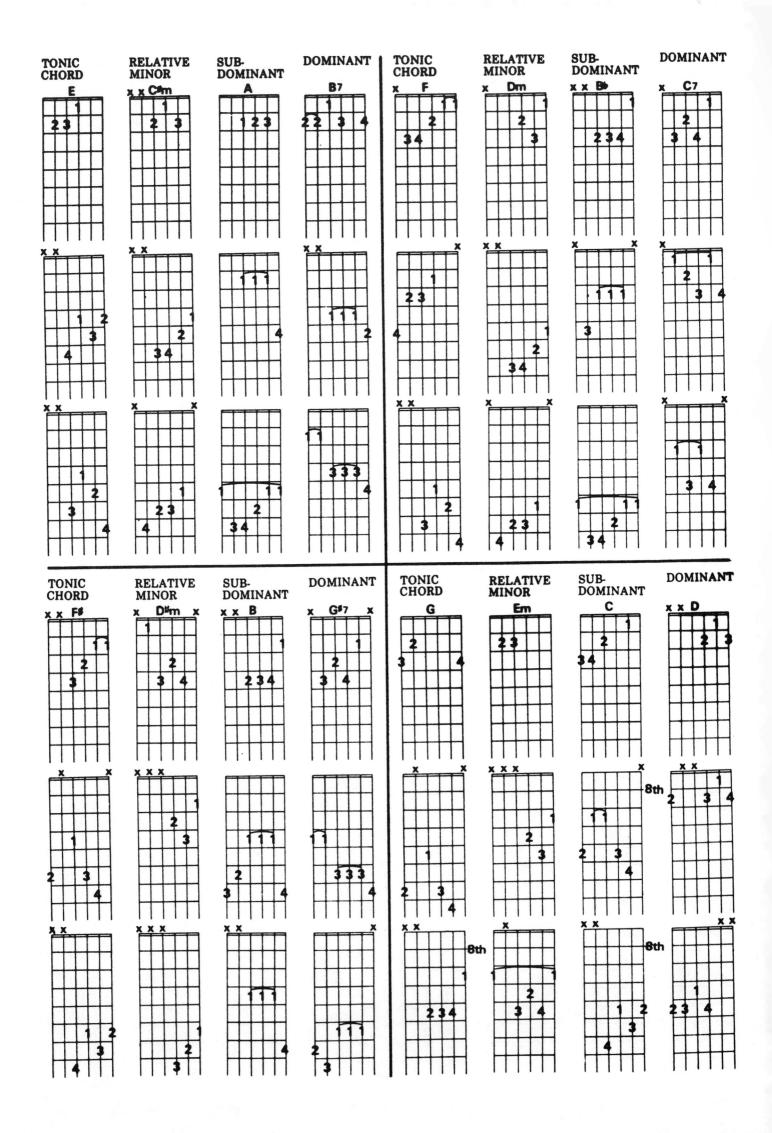

CHORD FORMULAS

Although I have set out a comprehensive chord bank to help you get started, you should always try to build chords for yourself and use the chord bank just to check that you're right. As I'm sure you guessed, there is a formula for every type of chord. Here they are.

MAJOR CHORDS

MAJOR	1	3	5			
MAJOR 6TH	1	3	5	6		
MAJOR 7TH	1	3	5	7		
MAJOR 9TH	1	3	5	7	9	
MAJOR 11TH	1	3	5	7	9	11
MAJOR 13TH	1	3	5	7	9	11	13

MINOR CHORDS

MINOR	1	♭3	5			
MINOR 6TH	1	♭3	5	6		
MINOR 7TH	1	♭3	5	♭7		
MINOR 9TH	1	♭3	5	♭7	9	
MINOR 11TH	1	♭3	5	♭7	9	11
MINOR 13TH	1	♭3	5	♭7	9	11	13

DOMINANT CHORDS

DOMINANT 7TH	1	3	5	♭7		
DOMINANT 9TH	1	3	5	♭7	9	
DOMINANT 11TH	1	3	5	♭7	9	11
DOMINANT 13TH	1	3	5	♭7	9	11	13

DIMINISHED CHORDS

DIMINISHED	1	♭3	♭5	
DIMINISHED 6TH	1	♭3	♭5	6
DIMINISHED 7TH	1	♭3	♭5	♭♭7

AUGMENTED CHORDS

AUGMENTED	1	3	♯5			
AUGMENTED 7TH	1	3	♯5	♭7		
AUGMENTED 9TH	1	3	♯5	♭7	9	
AUGMENTED 11TH	1	3	♯5	♭7	9	11
AUGMENTED 13TH	1	3	♯5	♭7	9	11	13

If you would like to be put on the mailing list to receive information on
future STRINGALONG publications, etc., please write to us at
STRINGALONG, CENTER VALLEY, PA   18034